Unit 1 Concepts of Managerial Economics

⊚	**Learning Outcome**

After going through this unit, you will be able to:

- Explain succinctly the meaning and definition of managerial economics

- Elucidate on the characteristics and scope of managerial economics

- Describe the techniques of managerial economics

- Explain the application of managerial economics in various aspects of decision making

- Explicate the application of managerial economics in marginal analysis and optimisation

🕐	**Time Required to Complete the unit**

1. 1st Reading: It will need 3 Hrs for reading a unit

2. 2nd Reading with understanding: It will need 4 Hrs for reading and understanding a unit

3. Self Assessment: It will need 3 Hrs for reading and understanding a unit

4. Assignment: It will need 2 Hrs for completing an assignment

5. Revision and Further Reading: It is a continuous process

🔍	**Content Map**

1.1 Introduction

1.2 **Concept of Managerial Economics**

   1.2.1 Meaning of Managerial Economics

   1.2.2 Definitions of Managerial Economics

1.2.3   Characteristics of Managerial Economics

1.2.4   Scope of Managerial Economics

1.2.5   Why Managers Need to Know Economics?

1.3   Techniques of Managerial Economics

1.4   Managerial Economics - Its application in Marginal Analysis and Optimisation

1.4.1   Application of Managerial Economics

1.4.2   Tools of Decision Science and Managerial Economics

1.5   Summary

1.6   Self Assessment Test

1.7   Further Reading

1.1   Introduction

Managerial decisions are an important cog in the working wheel of an organisation. The success or failure of a business is contingent upon the decisions taken by managers. Increasing complexity in the business world has spewed forth greater challenges for managers. Today, no business decision is bereft of influences from areas other than the economy. Decisions pertinent to production and marketing of goods are shaped with a view of the world both inside as well as outside the economy. Rapid changes in technology, greater focus on innovation in products as well as processes that command influence over marketing and sales techniques have contributed to the escalating complexity in the business environment. This complex environment is coupled with a global market where input and product prices are have a propensity to fluctuate and remain volatile. These factors work in tandem to increase the difficulty in precisely evaluating and determining the outcome of a business decision. Such evanescent environments give rise to a pressing need for sound economic analysis prior to making decisions. Managerial economics is a discipline that is designed to facilitate a solid foundation of economic understanding for business managers and enable them to make informed and analysed managerial decisions, which are in keeping with the transient and complex business environment.

1.2 Concept of Managerial Economics

The discipline of managerial economics deals with aspects of economics and tools of analysis, which are employed by business enterprises for decision-making. Business and industrial enterprises have to undertake varied decisions that entail managerial issues and decisions. Decision-making can be delineated as a process where a particular course of action is chosen from a number of alternatives. This demands an unclouded perception of the technical and environmental conditions, which are integral to decision making. The decision maker must possess a thorough knowledge of aspects of economic theory and its tools of analysis. The basic concepts of decision-making theory have been culled from microeconomic theory and have been furnished with new tools of analysis. Statistical methods, for example, are pivotal in estimating current and future demand for products. The methods of operations research and programming proffer scientific criteria for maximising profit, minimising cost and determining a viable combination of products.

Decision-making theory and game theory, which recognise the conditions of uncertainty and imperfect knowledge under which business managers operate, have contributed to systematic methods of assessing investment opportunities.

Almost any business decision can be analysed with managerial economics techniques. However, the most frequent applications of these techniques are as follows:

- **Risk analysis:** Various models are used to quantify risk and asymmetric information and to employ them in decision rules to manage risk.

- **Production analysis:** Microeconomic techniques are used to analyse production efficiency, optimum factor allocation, costs and economies of scale. They are also utilised to estimate the firm's cost function.

- **Pricing analysis:** Microeconomic techniques are employed to examine various pricing decisions. This involves transfer pricing, joint product pricing, price discrimination, price elasticity estimations and choice of the optimal pricing method.

- **Capital budgeting:** Investment theory is used to scrutinise a firm's capital purchasing decisions.

1.2.1 MEANING OF MANAGERIAL ECONOMICS

Managerial economics, used synonymously with business economics, is a branch of economics that deals with the application of microeconomic analysis to decision-making techniques of businesses and management units. It acts as the via media between economic theory and pragmatic economics. Managerial economics bridges the gap between 'theoria' and 'pracis'. The tenets of managerial economics have been derived from quantitative techniques such as regression analysis, correlation and Lagrangian calculus (linear). An omniscient and unifying theme found in managerial economics is the attempt to achieve optimal results from business decisions, while taking into account the firm's objectives, constraints imposed by scarcity and so on. A paradigm of such optmisation is the use of operations research and programming.

Managerial economics is thereby a study of application of managerial skills in economics. It helps in anticipating, determining and resolving potential problems or obstacles. These problems may pertain to costs, prices, forecasting future market, human resource management, profits and so on.

1.2.2 DEFINITIONS OF MANAGERIAL ECONOMICS

McGutgan and Moyer: "Managerial economics is the application of economic theory and methodology to decision-making problems faced by both public and private institutions".

McNair and Meriam: "Managerial economics consists of the use of economic modes of thought to analyse business situations".

Spencer and Siegelman: Managerial economics is "the integration of economic theory with business practice for the purpose of facilitating decision-making and forward planning by management".

Haynes, Mote and Paul: "Managerial economics refers to those aspects of economics and its tools of analysis most relevant to the firm's decision-making process". By definition, therefore, its scope does not extend to macro-economic theory and the economics of public policy, an understanding of which is also essential for the manager.

Managerial economics studies the application of the principles, techniques and concepts of economics to managerial problems of business and industrial enterprises. The term is used interchangeably with business economics, microeconomics, economics of enterprise, applied economics, managerial analysis and so on. Managerial economics lies at the junction of economics and business management and traverses the hiatus between the two disciplines.

Economics -Theory and Methodology		Business Management -Decision Problems
	Managerial Economics -Application of Economics to solve business problems	

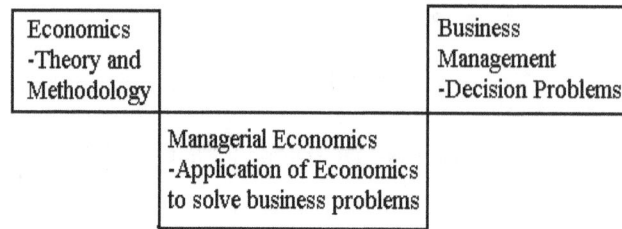

Chart: Economics, Business Management and Managerial Economics

Fig. 1.1: Relation between Economics Business Management and Managerial Economics

1.2.3 CHARACTERISTICS OF MANAGERIAL ECONOMICS

1. **Microeconomics:** It studies the problems and principles of an individual business firm or an individual industry. It aids the management in forecasting and evaluating the trends of the market.

2. **Normative economics:** It is concerned with varied corrective measures that a management undertakes under various circumstances. It deals with goal determination, goal development and achievement of these goals. Future planning, policy-making, decision-making and optimal utilisation of available resources, come under the banner of managerial economics.

3. **Pragmatic:** Managerial economics is pragmatic. In pure micro-economic theory, analysis is performed, based on certain exceptions, which are far from reality. However, in managerial economics, managerial issues are resolved daily and difficult issues of economic theory are kept at bay.

4. **Uses theory of firm:** Managerial economics employs economic concepts and principles, which are known as the theory of Firm or 'Economics of the Firm'. Thus, its scope is narrower than that of pure economic theory.

5. **Takes the help of macroeconomics:** Managerial economics incorporates certain aspects of macroeconomic theory. These are essential to comprehending the circumstances and environments that envelop the working conditions of an individual firm or an industry. Knowledge of macroeconomic issues such as business cycles, taxation policies, industrial policy of the government, price and distribution policies, wage policies and anti-monopoly policies and so on, is integral to the successful functioning of a business

enterprise.

6. **Aims at helping the management**: Managerial economics aims at supporting the management in taking corrective decisions and charting plans and policies for future.

7. **A scientific art:** Science is a system of rules and principles engendered for attaining given ends. Scientific methods have been credited as the optimal path to achieving one's goals. Managerial economics has been is also called a scientific art because it helps the management in the best and efficient utilisation of scarce economic resources. It considers production costs, demand, price, profit, risk etc. It assists the management in singling out the most feasible alternative. Managerial economics facilitates good and result oriented decisions under conditions of uncertainty.

8. **Prescriptive rather than descriptive:** Managerial economics is a normative and applied discipline. It suggests the application of economic principles with regard to policy formulation, decision-making and future planning. It not only describes the goals of an organisation but also prescribes the means of achieving these goals.

1.2.4 SCOPE OF MANAGERIAL ECONOMICS

The scope of managerial economics includes following subjects:

1. Theory of demand

2. Theory of production

3. Theory of exchange or price theory

4. Theory of profit

5. Theory of capital and investment

6. Environmental issues, which are enumerated as follows:

1. **Theory of Demand:** According to Spencer and Siegelman, "A business firm is an economic organisation which transforms productivity sources into goods that are to be sold in a market".

   a. **Demand analysis:** Analysis of demand is undertaken to forecast demand, which is a fundamental component in managerial decision-making. Demand forecasting is of importance because an estimate of future sales is a primer for preparing production schedule and employing productive resources. Demand analysis helps the management in identifying factors that influence the demand for the products of a firm. Thus, demand analysis and forecasting is of prime importance to business planning.

b. **Demand theory:** Demand theory relates to the study of consumer behaviour. It addresses questions such as what incites a consumer to buy a particular product, at what price does he/she purchase the product, why do consumers cease consuming a commodity and so on. It also seeks to determine the effect of the income, habit and taste of consumers on the demand of a commodity and analyses other factors that influence this demand.

2. **Theory of Production:** Production and cost analysis is central for the unhampered functioning of the production process and for project planning. Production is an economic activity that makes goods available for consumption. Production is also defined as a sum of all economic activities besides consumption. It is the process of creating goods or services by utilising various available resources. Achieving a certain profit requires the production of a certain amount of goods. To obtain such production levels, some costs have to be incurred. At this point, the management is faced with the task of determining an optimal level of production where the average cost of production would be minimum. Production function shows the relationship between the quantity of a good/service produced (output) and the factors or resources (inputs) used. The inputs employed for producing these goods and services are called factors of production.

a. **Variable factor of production:** The input level of a variable factor of production can be varied in the short run. Raw material inputs are deemed as variable factors. Unskilled labour is also considered in the category of variable factors.

b. **Fixed factor of production:** The input level of a fixed factor cannot be varied in the short run. Capital falls under the category of a fixed factor. Capital alludes to resources such as buildings, machinery etc.

Production theory facilitates in determining the size of firm and the level of production. It elucidates the relationship between average and marginal costs and production. It highlights how a change in production can bring about a parallel change in average and marginal costs. Production theory also deals with other issues such as conditions leading to increase or decrease in costs, changes in total production when one factor of production is varied and others are kept constant, substitution of one factor with another while keeping all increased simultaneously and methods of achieving optimum production.

3. **Theory of Exchange or Price Theory:** Theory of Exchange is popularly known as Price Theory. Price determination under different types of market conditions comes under the wingspan of this theory. It helps in determining the level to which an advertisement can be used to boost market sales of a firm. Price theory is pivotal in determining the price policy of a firm. Pricing is an important area in managerial economics. The accuracy of pricing decisions is vital in shaping the success of an enterprise. Price policy impresses upon the demand of products. It involves the determination of prices under different market conditions, pricing methods, pricing policies, differential pricing, product line pricing and price forecasting.

4. **Theory of profit:** Every business and industrial enterprise aims at maximising profit. Profit is the difference between total revenue and total economic cost. Profitability of an organisation is greatly influenced by the following factors:
   - Demand of the product
   - Prices of the factors of production
   - Nature and degree of competition in the market
   - Price behaviour under changing conditions

   Hence, profit planning and profit management are important requisites for improving profit earning efficiency of the firm. Profit management involves the use of most efficient technique for predicting the future. The probability of risks should be minimised as far as possible.

5. **Theory of Capital and Investment:** Theory of Capital and Investment evinces the following important issues:
   - Selection of a viable investment project
   - Efficient allocation of capital

- Assessment of the efficiency of capital

- Minimising the possibility of under capitalisation or overcapitalisation. Capital is the building block of a business. Like other factors of production, it is also scarce and expensive. It should be allocated in most efficient manner.

6. **Environmental issues:** Managerial economics also encompasses some aspects of macroeconomics. These relate to social and political environment in which a business and industrial firm has to operate. This is governed by the following factors:

- The type of economic system of the country

- Business cycles

- Industrial policy of the country

- Trade and fiscal policy of the country

- Taxation policy of the country

- Price and labour policy

- General trends in economy concerning the production, employment, income, prices, saving and investment etc.

- General trends in the working of financial institutions in the country

- General trends in foreign trade of the country

- Social factors like value system of the society

- General attitude and significance of social organisations like trade unions, producers' unions and consumers' cooperative societies etc.

- Social structure and class character of various social groups

- Political system of the country

The management of a firm cannot exercise control over these factors. Therefore, it should fashion the plans, policies and programmes of the firm according to these factors in order to offset their adverse effects on the firm.

1.2.5 WHY MANAGERS NEED TO KNOW ECONOMICS

The contribution of economics towards the performance of managerial duties and responsibilities is of prime importance. The contribution and importance of economics to the managerial profession is akin to the contribution of biology to the medical profession and physics to engineering. It has been observed that managers equipped with a working knowledge of economics surpass their otherwise equally qualified peers, who lack knowledge of economics. Managers are responsible for achieving the objective of the firm to the maximum possible extent with the limited resources placed at their disposal. It is important to note that maximisation of objective has to be achieved by utilising limited resources. In the event of resources being unlimited, like air or sunshine, the problem of economic utilisation of resources or resource management would not have arisen. Resources like finance, workforce and material are limited. However, in the absence of unlimited resources, it is the responsibility of the management to optimise the use of these resources.

- **How economics contributes to managerial functions**

Though economics is variously defined, it is essentially the study of logic, tools and techniques, to make optimum use of the available resources to achieve the given ends. Economics affords analytical tools and techniques that managers require to accomplish the goals of the organisation they manage. Therefore, a working knowledge of economics, not necessarily a formal degree, is indispensable for managers. Managers are fundamentally practicing economists.

While executing his duties, a manager has to take several decisions, which conform to the objectives of the firm. Many business decisions fall prey to conditions of uncertainty and risk. Uncertainty and risk arise chiefly due to volatile market forces, changing business environment, emerging competitors with highly competitive products, government policy, external influences on the domestic market and social and political changes in the country. The intricacy of the modern business world weaves complexity in to the decision making process of a business. However, the degree of uncertainty and risk can be greatly condensed if market conditions are calculated with a high degree of reliability. Envisaging a business environment in the future does not suffice. Appropriate business decisions and formulation of a business strategy in conformity with the goals of the firm hold similar importance.

Pertinent business decisions require an unambiguous understanding of the technical and environmental conditions under which business decisions are taken. Application of economic theories to explain and analyse technical conditions and business environment, contributes greatly to the rational decision-making process. Economic theories have many pronged applications in the analysis of practical problems of business. Keeping in view the escalating complexity of business environment, the efficacy of economic theory as a tool of analysis and its contribution to the process of decision-making has been widely recognised.

- Contributions of economic theory to business economics

According to Baumol, there are three main contributions of economic theory to business economics.

1. The practice of building analytical models, which assist in recognising the structure of

managerial problems and eliminating minor details, which might obstruct decision-making has been derived from economic theory. Analytical models help in eradicating peripheral problems and help the management in retaining focus on core issues.

2. Economic theory comprises a founding pillar of business analysis- 'a set of analytical methods', which may not be applied directly to specific business problems, but they do enhance the analytical capabilities of the business analyst.

3. Economic theories offer an unequivocal perspective on the various concepts used in business analysis, which enables the manager to swerve from conceptual pitfalls.

- **Importance of managerial economics**

Business and industrial enterprises aim at earning maximum proceeds. In order to achieve this objective, a managerial executive has to take recourse in decision-making, which is the process of selecting a specified course of action from a number of alternatives. A sound decision requires fair knowledge of the aspects of economic theory and the tools of economic analysis, which are directly involved in the process of decision-making. Since managerial economics is concerned with such aspects and tools of analysis, it is pertinent to the decision-making process.

Spencer and Siegelman have described the importance of managerial economics in a business and industrial enterprise as follows:

1. **Accommodating traditional theoretical concepts to the actual business behaviour and conditions:** Managerial economics amalgamates tools, techniques, models and theories of traditional economics with actual business practices and with the environment in which a firm has to operate. According to Edwin Mansfield, "Managerial Economics attempts to bridge the gap between purely analytical problems that intrigue many economic theories and the problems of policies that management must face".

2. **Estimating economic relationships:** Managerial economics estimates economic relationships between different business factors such as income, elasticity of demand, cost volume, profit analysis etc.

3. **Predicting relevant economic quantities:** Managerial economics assists the management in predicting various economic quantities such as cost, profit, demand, capital, production, price etc. As a business manager has to function in an environment of uncertainty, it is imperative to anticipate the future working environment in terms of the said quantities.

4. **Understanding significant external forces:** The management has to identify all the important factors that influence a firm. These factors can broadly be divided into two categories. Managerial economics plays an important role by assisting management in understanding these factors.

- **External factors:** A firm cannot exercise any control over these factors. The plans, policies and programmes of the firm should be formulated in the light of these factors. Significant external factors impinging on the decision-making process of a firm are economic system of the country, business cycles, fluctuations in national income and national production, industrial policy of the government, trade and fiscal policy of the government, taxation policy, licensing policy, trends in foreign trade of the country, general industrial relation in the country and so on.
- **Internal factors:** These factors fall under the control of a firm. These factors are associated with business operation. Knowledge of these factors aids the management in making sound business decisions.

5. **Basis of business policies:** Managerial economics is the founding principle of business policies. Business policies are prepared based on studies and findings of managerial economics, which cautions the management against potential upheavals in national as well as international economy.

Thus, managerial economics is helpful to the management in its decision-making process.

🔔	**Study Notes**

👁	**Assessment**

Answer the followings in detail:

1. What do you understand by Managerial Economics? Give Definition and meaning of Managerial Economics.

2. What are the characteristics and scope of Managerial Economics?

	Discussion
What is the relation between Economics, Business Management and Managerial Economics? Discuss.	

1.3   Techniques of Managerial Economics

Managerial economics draws on a wide variety of economic concepts, tools and techniques in the decision-making process. These concepts can be categorised as follows: (1) the theory of the firm, which explains how businesses make a variety of decisions; (2) the theory of consumer behavior, which describes the consumer's decision-making process and (3) the theory of market structure and pricing, which describes the structure and characteristics of different market forms under which business firms operate.

1. **Theory of the firm:** A firm can be considered an amalgamation of people, physical and financial resources and a variety of information. Firms exist because they perform useful functions in society by producing and distributing goods and services. In the process of accomplishing this, they employ society's scarce resources, provide employment and pay taxes. If economic activities of society can be simply put into two categories- production and consumption- firms are considered the most basic economic entities on the production side, while consumers form the basic economic entities on the consumption side. The behaviour of firms is usually analysed in the context of an economic model, which is an idealised version of a real-world firm. The basic economic model of a business enterprise is called the theory of the firm.

2. **Theory of consumer behaviour:** The role of consumers in an economy is of vital importance since consumers spend most of their incomes on goods and services produced by firms. Consumers consume what firms produce. Thus, study of the theory of consumer behaviour is accorded importance. It is desirous to know the ultimate objective of a consumer. Economists have an optimisation model for consumers, which is analogous to that applied to firms or producers. While it is assumed that firms attempt at maximising profits, similarly there is an assumption that consumers attempt at

maximising their utility or satisfaction. While more goods and services provide greater utility to a consumer, however, consumers, like firms, are subject to constraints. Their consumption and choices are limited by a number of factors, including the amount of disposable income (the residual income after income taxes are paid for). A consumer's choice to consume is described by economists within a theoretical framework usually termed the theory of demand.

3. **Theories associated with different market structures:** A firms profit maximising output decisions take into account the market structure under which they are operate. There are four kinds of market organisations: perfect competition, monopolistic competition, oligopoly and monopoly.

All the above theories are analysed with the help a vast and varied quantitative tools and techniques.

!	**Study Notes**

👁	**Assessment**
What are the tools and techniques of Managerial Economics?	

1.4 Managerial Economics - Its application in Marginal Analysis and Optimisation

1.4.1 APPLICATION OF MANAGERIAL ECONOMICS

Tools of managerial economics can be used to achieve virtually all the goals of a business organisation in an efficient manner. Typical managerial decision-making may involve one of the following issues:

- Decisions pertaining to the price of a product and the quantity of the commodity to be produced

- Decisions regarding manufacturing product/part/component or outsourcing to/purchasing from another manufacturer

- Choosing the production technique to be employed in the production of a given product

- Decisions relating to the level of inventory of a product or raw material a firm will maintain

- Decisions regarding the medium of advertising and the intensity of the advertising campaign

- Decisions pertinent to employment and training

- Decisions regarding further business investment and the modes of financing the investment

It should be noted that the application of managerial economics is not restricted to profit-seeking business organisations. Tools of managerial economics can be applied equally well to decision problems of nonprofit organisations. Mark Hirschey and James L. Pappas cite the example of a nonprofit hospital making use of the managerial economics techniques for optimisation of resource use. While a nonprofit hospital is not like a typical firm seeking to maximise its profits, a hospital does strive to provide its patients the best medical care possible given its limited staff (doctors, nurses and support staff), equipment, space and other resources. The hospital administrator can employ concepts and tools of managerial economics to determine the optimal allocation of the limited resources available to the hospital. In addition to nonprofit business organisations, government agencies and other nonprofit organisations (such as cooperatives, schools and museums) can exploit the techniques of managerial decision making to achieve goals in the most efficient manner.

While managerial economics aids in making optimal decisions, one should be aware that it only describes the predictable economic consequences of a managerial decision. For example, tools of managerial economics can explain the effects of imposing automobile import quotas on the availability of domestic cars, prices charged for automobiles and the extent of competition in the auto industry. Analysis of managerial economics reveals that fewer cars will be available, prices of automobiles will increase and the extent of competition will be reduced. However, managerial economics does not address whether imposing automobile import quotas is a good government policy. This question encompasses broader political considerations involving what economists call value judgments.

1.4.2 TOOLS OF DECISION SCIENCE AND MANAGERIAL ECONOMICS

Managerial decision-making draws on economic concepts as well as tools and techniques of analysis provided by decision sciences. The major categories of these tools and techniques are optimisation, statistical estimation, forecasting, numerical analysis and game theory. Most of these methodologies are technical. The first three are briefly explained below to illustrate how tools of decision sciences are used in managerial decision-making.

1. Optimisation: Optimisation techniques are probably the most crucial to managerial decision making. Given that alternative courses of action are available, the manager attempts to produce the most optimal decision, consistent with stated managerial objectives. Thus, an optimisation problem can be stated as maximising an objective (called the objective function by mathematicians) subject to specified constraints. In determining the output level consistent with the maximum profit, the firm maximises profits, constrained by cost and capacity considerations. While a manager does not resolve the optimisation problem, he or she may make use of the results of mathematical analysis. In the profit maximisation example, the profit maximising condition requires that the firm select the production level at which marginal revenue equals marginal cost. This condition is obtained from an optimisation model/technique. The techniques of optimisation employed depend on the problem a manager is trying to solve.

2. **Statistical estimation:** A number of statistical techniques are used to estimate economic variables of interest to a manager. In some cases, statistical estimation techniques employed are simple. In other cases, they are much more complex and advanced. Thus, a manager may want to know the average price received by his competitors in the industry, as well as the standard deviation (a measure of variation across units) of the product price under consideration. In this case, the simple statistical concepts of mean (average) and standard deviation are used.

Estimating a relationship among variables requires a more advanced statistical technique. For example, a firm may desire to estimate its cost function i.e. the relationship between cost concept and the level of output. A firm may also wish to the demand function of its product that is the relationship between the demand for its product and factors that influence it. The estimates of costs and demand are usually based on data supplied by the firm. The statistical estimation technique employed is called regression analysis and is used to engender a mathematical model showing how a set of variables are related. This mathematical relationship can also be used to generate forecasts.

An example from the automobile industry is befitting for illustrating the forecasting method that employs simple regression analysis. Let us assume that a statistician has data on sales of American-made automobiles in the United States for the last 25 years. He or she has also determined that the sale of automobiles is related to the real disposable income of individuals. The statistician also has available the time series data (for the last 25 years) on real disposable income. Assume that the relationship between the time series on sales of American-made automobiles and the real disposable income of consumers is actually linear and it can thus be represented by a straight line. A rigorous mathematical technique is used to locate the straight line that most accurately represents the relationship between the time series on auto sales and disposable income.

3. **Forecasting:** It is a method or a technique to predict many future aspects of a business or any other operation. For example, a retailing firm that has been in business for the last 25 years may be interested in forecasting the likely sales volume for the coming year. Numerous forecasting techniques can be used to accomplish this goal. A forecasting technique, for example, can provide such a projection based on the experience of the firm during the last 25 years; that is, this forecasting technique bases the future forecast on the past data.

While the term 'forecasting' may appear technical, planning for the future is a critical aspect of managing any organisation or a business. The long-term success of any organisation has close association with the propensity of the management of the organisation to foresee its future and develop appropriate strategies to deal with the likely future scenarios. Intuition, good judgment and knowledge of economic conditions enables the manager to 'feel' or perhaps anticipate the likelihood in the future. It is not easy, however, to metamorphose a feeling about the future outcome into concrete data for instance, as a projection for next year's sales volume. Forecasting methods can help predict many future aspects of a business operation, such as forthcoming years' sales volume projections.

Suppose a forecast expert has been asked to provide quarterly estimates of the sales volume for a particular product for the next four quarters. How should he attempt at preparing the quarterly sales volume forecasts? Reviewing the actual sales data for the product in question for past periods will give a good start. Suppose that the forecaster has access to actual sales data for each quarter during the 25-year period the firm has been in business. Employing this historical data, the forecaster can identify the general trend of sales. He or she can also determine whether there is a pattern or trend, such as an increase or decrease in sales volume over time. An in depth review of the data may unearth some type of seasonal pattern, such as, peak sales occurring around the holiday season. Thus, by reviewing historical data, there is a high probability that the forecaster develops a good understanding of the pattern of sales in the past periods. Understanding such patterns can result in better forecasts of future sales of the product. In addition, if the forecaster is able to identify the factors that influence sales, historical data on these factors (variables) can also be used to generate forecasts of future sales.

There are many forecasting techniques available to the person assisting the business in planning its sales. Take for example a forecasting method in which a statistician forecasting future values of a variable of business interest—sales, for example, examines the cause-and-effect relationships of this variable with other relevant variables. The other pertinent variable may be the level of consumer confidence, changes in consumers' disposable incomes, the interest rate at which consumers can finance their excess spending through borrowing and the state of the economy represented by the percentage of the labour force unemployed. This category of forecasting technique utilises time series data on many relevant variables to forecast the volume of sales in the future. Under this forecasting technique, a regression equation is estimated to generate future forecasts (based on the past relationship among variables).

⚠	**Study Notes**

👁	**Assessment**
1. Explain how Managerial Economics is applied in Marginal Analysis?	
2. Explain Optimization.	

🗣	**Discussion**
Discuss Forecasting as a tool OF DECISION SCIENCE AND MANAGERIAL ECONOMICS.	

1.5 Summary

Managerial Economics: The discipline of managerial economics deals with aspects of economics and tools of analysis, which are employed by business enterprises for decision making. Business and industrial enterprises have to undertake varied decisions that entail managerial issues and decisions. Decision-making can be delineated as a process where a particular course of action is chosen from a number of alternatives. This demands an unclouded perception of the technical and environmental conditions, which are integral to decision making. The decision maker must possess a thorough knowledge of aspects of economic theory and its tools of analysis, which are integral to decision making. The basic concepts have been culled from microeconomic theory and have been furnished with new tools of analysis.

Characteristics of Managerial Economics: Following are the characteristics of managerial economics:

- Microeconomics

- Normative economics

- Pragmatic

- Uses theory of firm

- Takes the help of macroeconomics

- Aims at helping the management

- A scientific art

- Prescriptive rather than descriptive

Scope of managerial economics: The scope of managerial economics includes following subjects: 1) Theory of Demand 2) Theory of Production 3) Theory of Exchange or Price Theory 4) Theory of Profit 5) Theory of Capital and Investment 6) Environmental Issues

Importance of managerial economics: Spencer and Siegelman have described the importance of managerial economics in a business and industrial enterprise as follows:

- Reconciling traditional theoretical concepts to the actual business behaviour and conditions

- Estimating economic relationships

- Predicting relevant economic quantities

- Understanding significant external forces

- Basis of business policies

Techniques of managerial economics: Managerial economics uses a wide variety of economic concepts, tools and techniques in the decision-making process. These concepts can be enlisted as follows:

- The theory of the firm, which elucidates how businesses make a variety of decisions

- The theory of consumer behaviour, which describes decision making by consumers

- The theory of market structure and pricing, which opens a window into the structure and characteristics of different market forms under which business firms operate

1.6 Self Assessment Test

Broad Questions

1. Explain concept and techniques of managerial economics.

2. How is Managerial Economics applied in analysis and decision-making?

3. Why managers need to know economics? Explain the importance of managerial economics.

Short Notes

    a. Meaning and definition of managerial economics

    b. Application of managerial economics

    c. Theories of managerial economics

    d. Characteristics of managerial economics

    e. Optimisation and forecasting in managerial economics

1.7   Further Reading

1. A Modern Micro Economics, Koutsoyiannis, Macmillan, 1991

2. Business Economics, Adhikary M, Excel Books, 2000

3. Economics Theory and Operations Analysis, Baumol W. J., Ed. 3, Prentice Hall Inc, 1996

4. Managerial Economics, Chopra O P., Tata McGraw Hill, 1985

5. Managerial Economics, Keat Paul G & Philips K Y Young, Prentice Hall, 1996

6. Economics Organisation and Management, Milgrom P and Roberts J, Prentice Hall Inc, 1992

7. Managerial Economics, Maheshwari Yogesh, Sultanchand & Sons, 2009

8. Managerial Economics, Varshney R L., Sultanchand & Sons, 2007

9. Managerial Economics, Suma Damodaran, Oxford, 2006

Assignment

- What are the principles of managerial economics? How far are these principles followed in present managerial economic scenarios?
- Why is demand estimation and forecast important for managerial decision- making?

_____

_____

_____

_____

_____

_____

_____

_____

_____

_____

_____

_____

_____

_____

_____

_____

_____

_____

_____

_____

Unit 2   Theory of Demand

⊚	**Learning Outcome**

After going through this unit, you will be able to:

- Explain meaning and concept of demand

- Elucidate on Law of Demand and Elasticity of Demand

- Identify Demand Functions

- List Determinant factors of Elasticity of Demand

- Carry out Demand Forecasting

🕐	**Time Required to Complete the unit**

1.	1st Reading: It will need 3 Hrs for reading a unit
2.	2nd Reading with understanding: It will need 4 Hrs for reading and understanding a unit
3.	Self Assessment: It will need 3 Hrs for reading and understanding a unit
4.	Assignment: It will need 2 Hrs for completing an assignment
5.	Revision and Further Reading: It is a continuous process

🔍	**Content Map**

2.1	**Introduction**
2.2	**Theory of Demand**
	2.2.1 Essentials of Demand
	2.2.2 Law of Demand
2.3	**Demand Function**

2.4	**Elasticity of Demand**
	2.4.1 Price Elasticity of Demand
	2.4.2 Point and Arc Elasticity of Demand
	2.4.3 Nature of Demand Curves and Elasticity
	2.4.4 Slope of the Demand Curve and Price Elasticity
	2.4.5 Price Elasticity and Marginal revenue
	2.4.6 Price Elasticity and Consumption Expenditure
	2.4.7 Cross-Elasticity of Demand
	2.4.8 Income Elasticity of Demand
2.5	**Determinants of Demand**
2.6	**Demand Forecasting**
	2.6.1 Demand Forecast and Sales Forecast
	2.6.2 Components of Demand Forecasting System
	2.6.3 Objectives of Demand Forecast
	2.6.4 Importance of Demand Forecast
	2.6.5 Methods of Demand Forecast
	2.6.6 Some demand forecasting methods
	2.6.7 Methods of Estimation
2.7	**Summary**
2.8	**Self Assessment Test**
2.9	**Further Reading**

2.1 Introduction

Demand theory evinces the relationship between the demand for goods and services. Demand theory is the building block of the demand curve- a curve that establishes a relationship between consumer demand and the amount of goods available. Demand is shaped by the availability of goods, as the quantity of goods increases in the market the demand and the equilibrium price for those goods decreases as a result.

Demand theory is one of the core theories of microeconomics and consumer behaviour. It attempts at answering questions regarding the magnitude of demand for a product or service based on its importance to human wants. It also attempts to assess how demand is impacted by changes in prices and income levels and consumers preferences/utility. Based on the perceived utility of goods and services to consumers, companies are able to adjust the supply available and the prices charged.

In economics, demand has a specific meaning distinct from its ordinary usage. In common language we treat 'demand' and 'desire' as synonymously. This is incongruent from its use in economics. In economics, demand refers to effective demand which implies three things:

- Desire for a commodity

- Sufficient money to purchase the commodity, rather the ability to pay

- Willingness to spend money to acquire that commodity

This substantiates that a want or a desire does not develop into a demand unless it is supported by the ability and the willingness to acquire it. For instance, a person may desire to own a scooter but unless he has the required amount of money with him and the willingness to spend that amount on the purchase of a scooter, his desire shall not become a demand. The following should also be noted about demand:

- Demand always alludes to demand at price. The term 'demand' has no meaning unless it is related to price. For instance, the statement, 'the weekly demand for potatoes in city X is 10,000 kilograms' has no meaning unless we specify the price at which this quantity is demanded.

- Demand always implies demand per unit of time. Therefore, it is vital to specify the period for which the commodity is demanded. For instance, the statement that demand for potatoes in city X at Rs. 8 per kilogram is 10,000 kilograms again has no meaning, unless we state the period for which the quantity is being demanded. A complete statement would therefore be as follows: 'The weekly demand for potatoes in city X at Rs. 8 per kilogram is 10,000 kilograms'. It is necessary to specify the period and the price because demand for a commodity will be different at different prices of that commodity and for different periods of time. Thus, we can define demand as follows:

"The demand for a commodity at a given price is the amount of it which will be bought per unit of time at that price".

2.2   Theory of Demand

2.2.1 ESSENTIALS OF DEMAND

1. **An Effective Need:** Effective need entails that there should be a need supported by the capacity and readiness to shell out. Hence, there are three basics of an effective need:

   a.   The individual should have a need to acquire a specific product.

   b.   He should have sufficient funds to pay for that product.

   c.   He should be willing to part with these resources for that commodity.

2. **A Specific Price:** A proclamation concerning the demand of a product without mentioning its price is worthless. For example, to state that the demand of cars is 10,000 is worthless, unless expressed that the demand of cars is 10,000 at a price of Rs. 4, 00,000 each.

3. **A Specific Time:** Demand must be assigned specific time. For example, it is an incomplete proclamation to state that the demand of air conditioners is 4,000 at the price of Rs. 12,800 each. The statement should be altered to say that the demand of air conditioners during summer is 4,000 at the price of Rs. 12,800 each.

4. **A Specific Place:** The demand must relate to a specific market as well. For example, every year in the town of Dehradun, the demand for school bags is 4,000 at a price of Rs. 200.

   Hence, the demand of a product is an effective need, which demonstrates the quantity of a product that will be bought at a specific price in a specific market at some stage in a specific period. Nevertheless, the significance of a specific market or place is not as significant as the price and time period for which demand is being measured.

2.2.2 LAW OF DEMAND

We have considered various factors that fashion the demand for a commodity. As explained the first and the most important factor that determines the demand of a commodity is its price. If all other factors (noted above) remain constant, it may be said that as the price of a commodity increases, its demand decreases and as the price of a commodity decreases its demand increases. This is a general behaviour observed in a market. This gives us the law of demand:

"The demand for a commodity increases with a fall in its price and decreases with a rise in its price, other things remaining the same".

The law of demand thus merely states that the price and demand of a commodity are inversely related, provided all other things remain unchanged or as economists put it *ceteris paribus*.

- **Assumptions of the Law of Demand**

The above statement of the law of demand, demonstrates that that this law operates only when all other things remain constant. These are then the assumptions of the law of demand. We can state the assumptions of the law of demand as follows:

1. **Income level should remain constant:** The law of demand operates only when the income level of the buyer remains constant. If the income rises while the price of the commodity does not fall, it is quite likely that the demand may increase. Therefore, stability in income is an essential condition for the operation of the law of demand.

2. **Tastes of the buyer should not alter:** Any alteration that takes place in the taste of the consumers will in all probability thwart the working of the law of demand. It often happens that when tastes or fashions change people revise their preferences. As a consequence, the demand for the commodity which goes down the preference scale of the consumers declines even though its price does not change.

3. **Prices of other goods should remain constant:** Changes in the prices of other goods often impinge on the demand for a particular commodity. If prices of commodities for which demand is inelastic rise, the demand for a commodity other than these in all probability will decline even though there may not be any change in its price. Therefore, for the law of demand to operate it is imperative that prices of other goods do not change.

4. **No new substitutes for the commodity:** If some new substitutes for a commodity appear in the market, its demand generally declines. This is quite natural, because with the availability of new substitutes some buyers will be attracted towards new products and the demand for the older product will fall even though price remains unchanged. Hence, the law of demand operates only when the market for a commodity is not threatened by new substitutes.

5. **Price rise in future should not be expected:** If the buyers of a commodity expect that its price will rise in future they raise its demand in response to an initial price rise. This behaviour of buyers violates the law of demand. Therefore, for the operation of the law of demand it is necessary that there must not be any expectations of price rise in the future.

6. **Advertising expenditure should remain the same:** If the advertising expenditure of a firm increases, the consumers may be tempted to buy more of its product. Therefore, the advertising expenditure on the good under consideration is taken to be constant.

Desire of a person to purchase a commodity is not his demand. He must possess adequate resources and must be willing to spend his resources to buy the commodity. Besides, the quantity demanded has always a reference to 'a price' and 'a unity of time'. The quantity demanded referred to 'per unit of time' makes it a flow concept. There may be some problems in applying this flow concept to the demand for durable consumer goods like house, car, refrigerators, etc. However, this apparent difficulty may be resolved by considering the total service of a durable good is not consumed at one point of time and its utility is not exhausted in a single use. The service of a durable good is consumed over time. At a time, only a part of its service is consumed. Therefore, the demand for the services of durable consumer goods may also be visualised as a demand per unit of time. However, this problem does not arise when the concept of demand is applied to total demand for a consumer durable. Thus, the demand for consumer goods also is a flow concept.

- **Demand Schedule**

The law of demand can be illustrated through a demand schedule. A demand schedule is a series of quantities, which consumers would like to buy per unit of time at different prices. To illustrate the law of demand, an imaginary demand schedule for tea is given in Table 2.1. It shows seven alternative prices and the corresponding quantities (number of cups of tea) demand per day. Each price has a unique quantity demanded, associated with it. As the price per cup of tea decreases, daily demand for tea increases, in accordance with the law of demand.

Table 2.1: Demand Schedule for Tea

Price per Cup of Tea (Rs.)	No. of Cups of Tea Demand per Consumer per Day	Symbols representing per Price-Quantity Combination
8	2	A
7	3	B
6	4	C
5	5	D
4	6	E
3	7	F
2	8	G

- **Demand Curve**

The law of demand can also be presented through a curve called demand curve. Demand curve is a locus of points showing various alterative price-quantity combinations. It shows the quantities of a commodity that consumers or users would buy at difference prices per unit of time under the assumptions of the law of demand. An individual demand curve for tea as given in Fig. 2.1 can be obtained by plotting the data give in Table 2.1.

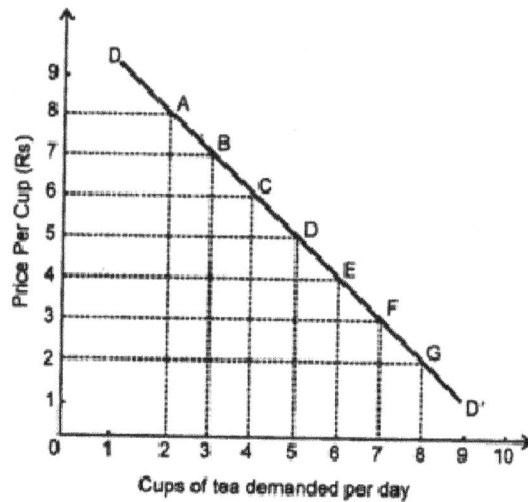

Fig.2.1: Demand Curve

In Fig. 2.1, the curve from point A to point G passing through points B, C, D and F is the demand curve DD'. Each point on the demand curve DD' shows a unique price-quantity combination. The combinations read in alphabetical order should decreasing price of tea and increasing number of cups of tea demanded per day. Price quantity combinations in reverse order of alphabets illustrate increasing price of tea per cup and decreasing number of cups of tea per day consumed by an individual. The whole demand curve shows a functional relationship between the alternative price of a commodity and its corresponding quantities, which a consumer would like to buy during a specific period of item—per day, per week, per month, per season, or per year. The demand curve shows an inverse relationship between price and quantity demanded. This inverse relationship between price and quantity demanded results in the demand curve sloping downward to the right.

- **Why does the demand curve slope downwards**

As Fig. 2.1 shows, demand curve slopes downward to the right. The downward slope of the demand curve reads the law of demand i.e. the quantity of a commodity demanded per unit of time increases as its price falls and vice versa.

The reasons behind the law of demand i.e. inverse relationship between price and quantity demanded are following:

- **Substitution Effect:** When the price of a commodity falls it becomes relatively cheaper if price of all other related goods, particularly of substitutes, remain constant. In other words, substitute goods become relatively costlier. Since consumers substitute cheaper goods for costlier ones, demand for the relatively cheaper commodity increases. The increase in demand on account of this factor is known as substitution effect.

- **Income Effect:** As a result of fall in the price of a commodity, the real income of its consumer increase at least in terms of this commodity. In other words, his/her purchasing power increases since he is required to pay less for the same quantity. The increase in real income (or purchasing power) encourages demand for the commodity with reduced price. The increase in demand on account of increase in real income is known as income effect. It should however be noted that the income effect is negative in case of inferior goods. In case, price of an inferior good accounting for a considerable proportion of the total consumption expenditure falls substantially, consumers' real income increases: they become relatively richer. Consequently, they substitute the superior good for the inferior ones, i.e., they reduce the consumption of inferior goods. Thus, the income effect on the demand for inferior goods becomes negative.

- **Diminishing Marginal Utility:** Diminishing marginal utility as well is to be held responsible for the rise in demand for a product when its price declines. When an individual purchases a product, he swaps his money revenue with the product in order to increase his satisfaction. He continues to purchase goods and services as long as the marginal utility of money (MU_m) is lesser than the marginal utility of the commodity (MU_c). Given the price of a commodity, he modifies his purchase so that $MU_c = MU_m$. This plan works well under both Marshallian assumption of constant MU_m as well as Hicksian assumption of diminishing MU_m. When price falls, ($MU_m = P_c$) < MU_c. Thus, equilibrium state is upset. To get back his equilibrium state, i.e., $MU_m = P_{c'} = MU_{c'}$, he buys more quantities of the commodity. For, when the supply of a commodity rises, its MU falls and once again $MU_m = MU_c$. For this reason, demand for a product rises when its price falls.

- **Exceptions to the Law of Demand**

    The law of demand does not apply to the following cases:

- **Apprehensions about the future price:** When consumers anticipate a constant rise in the price of a long-lasting commodity, they purchase more of it despite the price rise. They do so with the intention of avoiding the blow of still higher prices in the future. Likewise, when consumers expect a substantial fall in the price in the future, they delay their purchases and hold on for the price to decrease to the anticipated level instead of purchasing the commodity as soon as its price decreases. These kinds of choices made by the consumers are in contradiction of the law of demand.

- **Status goods:** The law does not concern the commodities which function as a 'status symbol', add to the social status or exhibit prosperity and opulence e.g. gold, precious stones, rare paintings and antiques, etc. Rich people mostly purchase such goods as they are very costly.

- **Giffen goods:** An exception to this law is the typical case of Giffen goods named after Sir Robert Giffen (1837-1910). 'Giffen goods' does not represent any particular commodity. It could be any low-grade commodity which is cheap as compared to its superior alternatives, consumed generally by the lower income group families as an important consumer good. If price of such goods rises (price of its alternative remaining stable), its demand escalates instead of falling. E.g. the minimum consumption of food grains by a lower income group family per month is 30 kgs consisting of 20 kgs of bajra (a low-grade good) at the rate of Rs 10 per kg and 10 kgs of wheat (a high quality good) at Rs. 20 per kg. They have a fixed expenditure of Rs. 400 on these items. However, if the price of bajra rises to Rs. 12 per kg the family will be compelled to decrease the consumption of wheat by 5 kgs and add to that of bajra by the same quantity so as to meet its minimum consumption requisite within Rs. 400 per month. No doubt, the family's demand for bajra rises from 20 to 25 kgs when its price rises.

- **The Market Demand Curve**

The quantity of a commodity which an individual is willing to buy at a particular price of the commodity during a specific time period, given his money income, his taste and prices of substitutes and complements, is known as individual demand for a commodity. The total quantity which all the consumers of a commodity are willing to buy at a given price per time unit, other things remaining the same, is known as market demand for the commodity. In other words, the market demand for a commodity is the sum of individual demands by all the consumers (or buyers) of the commodity, per time unit and at a given price, other factors remaining the same. For instance, suppose there are three consumers (viz., A, B, C) of a commodity X and their individual demand at different prices is of X as given in Table 2.2. The last column presents the market demand i.e. the aggregate of individual demand by three consumers at different prices.

Table 2.2: Price and Quantity Demanded

Price of Commodity X (Price per unit)	Quantity of X demanded by			Market Demand
	A	B	C	
10	4	2	0	6
8	8	4	0	12
6	12	6	2	20
4	16	8	4	28
2	20	10	6	36
0	24	12	8	44

Graphically, market demand curve is the horizontal summation of individual demand curves. The individual demand schedules plotted graphically and summed up horizontally gives the market demand curve as shown in Fig. 2.2.

The individual demands for commodity X are given by D_A, D_B and D_c, respectively. The horizontal summation of these individual demand curves results into the market demand curve (D_M) for the commodity X. The curve D_M represents the market demand curve for commodity X when there are only three consumers of the commodity.

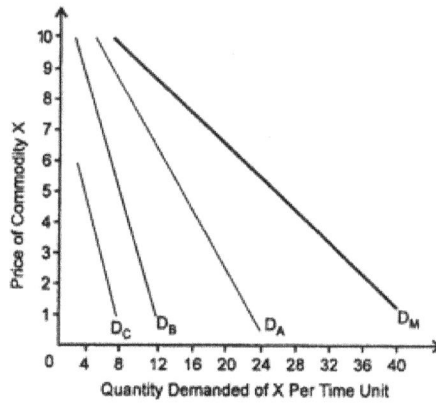

Fig. 2.2: Derivation of market demand

⚠	**Study Notes**

👁	**Assessment**
1.	What are the essentials of a Demand?
2.	Explain Law of Demand, in detail.

  Discussion
Why does the demand curve slope downwards? Discuss.

2.3   Demand Function

The functional relationship between the demand for a commodity and its various determinants may be expressed mathematically in terms of a demand function, thus:

Dx = f (Px, Py, M, T, A, U) where,

Dx = Quantity demanded for commodity X.

f = functional relation.

Px = The price of commodity X.

Py = The price of substitutes and complementary goods.

M = The money income of the consumer.

T = The taste of the consumer.

A = The advertisement effects.

U = Unknown variables or influences.

The above-stated demand function is a complicated one. Again, factors like tastes and unknown influences are not quantifiable. Economists, therefore, adopt a very simple statement of demand function, assuming all other variables, except price, to be constant. Thus, an over-simplified and the most commonly stated demand function is: Dx = f (Px), which connotes that the demand for commodity X is the function of its price. The traditional demand theory deals with this demand function specifically.

It must be noted that by demand function, economists mean the entire functional relationship i.e. the whole range of price-quantity relationship and not just the quantity demanded at a given price per unit of time. In other words, the statement, 'the quantity demanded is a function of price' implies that for every price there is a corresponding quantity demanded.

To put it differently, demand for a commodity means the entire demand schedule, which shows the varying amounts of goods purchased at alternative prices at a given time.

Shift in Demand Curve

When demand curve changes its position retaining its shape (though not necessarily), the change is known as shift in demand curve.

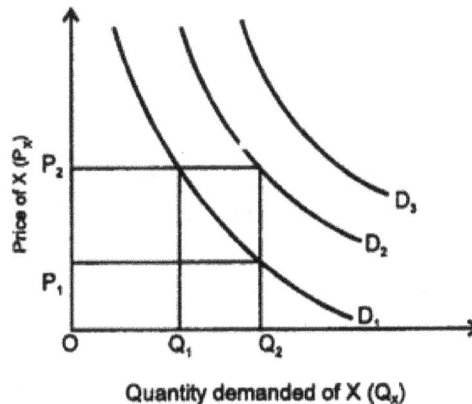

Fig 2.3: Shift in Demand Curves

Let's suppose that the demand curve D_2 in Fig. 2.3 is the original demand curve for commodity X. As shown in the figure, at price OP_2 consumer buys OQ_2 units of X, other factors remaining constant. If any of the other factors (e.g., consumer's income) changes, it will change the consumer's ability and willingness to buy commodity X. For example, if consumer's disposable income decreases, say, due to increase in income tax, he may be able to buy only OQ_1 units of X instead of OQ_2 at price OP_2 (This is true for the whole range of price of X) the consumers would be able to buy less of commodity X at all other prices. This will cause a downward shift in demand curve from D_2 to D_1. Similarly, increase in disposable income of the consumer due to reduction in taxes may cause an upward shift from D_2 to D_3. Such changes in the position of the demand curve are known as shifts in demand curve.

Reasons for Shift in Demand Curve

Shifts in a price-demand curve may take place owing to the change in one or more of other determinants of demand. Consider, for example, the decrease in demand for commodity X by Q_1Q_2 in Fig 2.3. Given the price OP_1, the demand for X might have fallen from OQ_2 to OQ_1 (i.e., by Q_1Q_2) for any of the following reasons:

• Fall in the consumer's income so that he can buy only OQ_1 of X at price OP_2—

  it is income effect.

• Price of X's substitute falls so that the consumers find it beneficial to substitute Q_1Q_2 of X with its substitute—it is substitution effect.

- Advertisement made by the producer of the substitute, changes consumer's taste or preference against commodity X so much that they replace Q_1Q_2 of X with its substitute, again a substitution effect.

- Price of complement of X increases so much that they can now afford only OQ_x of X

- Also for such reasons as commodity X is going out of fashion; its quality has deteriorated; consumer's technology has so changed that only OQ_1 of X can be used and due to change in season if commodity X has only seasonal use.

⚠	**Study Notes**

👁	**Assessment**
Explain, why there is shift in demand curve?	

🗣	**Discussion**
Give the functional relationship between the demand for a commodity and its various determinants, in mathematical terms of a demand function.	

2.4   Elasticity of Demand

While the law of demand establishes a relationship between price and quantity demanded for a product, it does not tell us exactly as how strong or weak the relationship happens to be. This relation, as already discussed, is inverse baring some rare exceptions. However, a manager needs an exact measure of this relationship for appropriate business decisions. Elasticity of demand is a measure, which comes to the rescue of a manager here. It measures the responsiveness of demand to changes in prices as well as changes in income. A manager can determine almost exactly how the demand for his product would change when he changes his price or when his rivals alter prices of their products. He can also determine how the demand for his product would change if incomes of his consumers go up or down. Elasticity of demand concept and its measurements are therefore very important tools of managerial decision making.

From decision-making point of view, however, the knowledge of only the nature of relationships is not sufficient. What is more important is the extent of relationship or the degree of responsiveness of demand to changes in its determinants. The responsiveness of demand for a good to the change in its determinants is called the elasticity of demand. The concept of elasticity of demand was introduced into the economic theory by Alfred Marshall. The elasticity concept plays an important role in various business decisions and government policies. In this unit, we will discuss the following kinds of demand elasticity.

- **Price Elasticity:** Elasticity of demand for a commodity with respect to change in its price.

- **Cross Elasticity:** Elasticity of demand for a commodity with respect to change in the price of its substitutes.

- **Income Elasticity:** Elasticity of demand with respect to change in consumer's income.

- **Price Expectation Elasticity of Demand:** Elasticity of demand with respect to consumer's expectations regarding future price of the commodity.

2.4.1 PRICE ELASTICITY OF DEMAND

The price elasticity of demand is delineated as the degree of responsiveness or sensitiveness of demand for a commodity to the changes in its price. More precisely, elasticity of demand is the percentage change in the quantity demanded of a commodity as a result of a certain percentage change in its price. A formal definition of price elasticity of demand (e) is given below:

$$e_p = \frac{\text{Percentage change in quantity demanded}}{\text{Percentage change in price}}$$

The measure of price elasticity (e) is called co-efficient of price elasticity. The measure of price elasticity is converted into a more general formula for calculating coefficient of price elasticity given as

$$e_p = -\frac{\Delta Q}{Q_o} \div \frac{\Delta P}{P_o} = -\frac{\Delta Q}{Q_o} \cdot \frac{P_o}{\Delta P}$$

$$= -\frac{\Delta Q}{\Delta P} \cdot \frac{P_o}{Q_o}$$

--eq. I

Where Q_o = original quantity demanded, P_o = original price, ▲Q = change in quantity demanded and ▲P = change in price.

Note that a minus sign (-) is generally inserted in the formula before the fraction with a view to making elasticity coefficient a non-negative value.

2.4.2 POINT AND ARC ELASTICITY OF DEMAND

The elasticity of demand is conventionally measured either at a finite point or between any two finite points, on the demand curve. The elasticity measured on a finite point of a demand curve is called point elasticity and the elasticity measured between any two finite points is called arc elasticity. Let us now look into the methods of measuring point and arc elasticity and their relative usefulness.

(A) POINT ELASTICITY

The point elasticity of demand is defined as the proportionate change in quantity demanded in response to a very small proportionate change in price. The concept of point elasticity is useful where change in price and the consequent change in quantity demanded are very small.

The point elasticity may be symbolically expressed as

$$e_p = -\frac{\partial Q}{\partial P} \cdot \frac{P}{Q}$$

--eq. II

Measuring Point Elasticity on a Linear Demand Curve

To illustrate the measurement of point elasticity of a linear demand curve, let us suppose that a linear demand curve is given by MN in Fig. 2.4 and that we want to measure elasticity at point P.

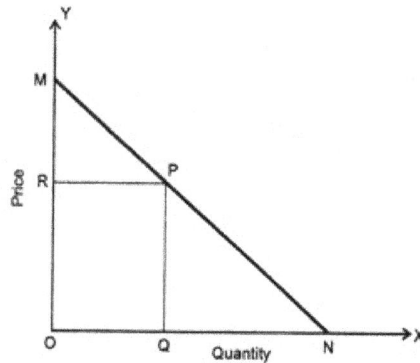

Fig. 2.4: Point Elasticity of a Linear Demand Curve

Let us now substitute the values from Fig. 2.4 in eq. II. As it is obvious from the figure, P = PQ and Q = OQ. What we need now is to find the values for δQ and δP. These values can be obtained by assuming a very small decrease in the price. However, it will be difficult to depict these changes in the figure as and hence Q –O. There is however an easier way to find the value for $\delta Q/\delta P$. In derivative given the slope of the demand curve MN. The slope of demand curve MN, at point P is geometrically given by QN/PQ. That is, may be proved as follows. If we draw a horizontal line from P and to the vertical -.here will be three triangles.

$$\frac{\partial Q}{\partial P} = \frac{QN}{PQ}$$

Since at point P, P=PQ and Q=OQ, substituting these values in eq. II, (ignoring the minus sign), we get

$$e_p = \frac{QN}{PQ} \cdot \frac{PQ}{OQ} = \frac{QN}{OQ}$$

Geometrically,

$$\frac{QN}{OQ} = \frac{PN}{PM}$$

▲MON, ▲MRP and ▲PQN (Fig. 3.1) in which ▲MON and ▲PQN are right angles. Therefore, the other corresponding angles of the triangles will always be equal and hence, ▲ MON, ▲MRP and ▲PQN are similar triangles.

According to geometrical properties of similar triangles, the ratio of any two sides of similar triangle is always equal to the ratio of corresponding sides of the other sides. Therefore, in ▲PQN and ▲MRP,

$$\frac{QN}{PN} = \frac{RP}{PM}$$ ……………………………… eq. III

Hence, RP=OQ, by substituting OQ for RP in eq. III, we get

$$\frac{QN}{PN} = \frac{OQ}{PM}$$

In proportionality rule, therefore,

$$\frac{QN}{OQ} = \frac{PN}{PM}$$

It may thus be concluded that price elasticity at point P (Fig 2.4) is given by

$$e_p = \frac{PN}{PM}$$

Measuring Point Elasticity on a Non-linear Demand Curve

Let us now elucidate the method of measuring point elasticity on a non-linear demand curve. Suppose we want to measure the elasticity of demand curve DD' at point P in, let us draw a line (MN) tangent to the demand curve DD' at point P. Since demand curve DD' and the line MN pass through the same point (P) the slope of demand curve and that of the line at this point is the same. Therefore, the elasticity of demand curve DD' at point P will be equal to the elasticity of demand line, MN, at point P. Elasticity of the line, MN, at point P can be measured (ignoring 'minus' sign) as

$$e_p = \frac{\text{Lower segment}}{\text{Upper segment}}$$

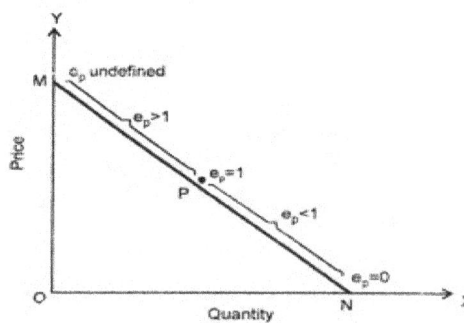

Fig 2.5: Point Elasticity of Demand

Managerial Economics

Given the graphical measurement of point elasticity, it is obvious that the elasticity at a point of a demand curve is the ratio between the lower and the upper segments of a linear demand curve from the point chosen for measuring point elasticity. That is,

$$e_p = \frac{\partial Q}{\partial P} \cdot \frac{P}{Q}$$

$$\frac{QN}{PQ} \cdot \frac{PQ}{OQ} = \frac{QN}{OQ}$$

Geometrically, QN/OQ=PN/PM. (For proof, see the proceeding section).

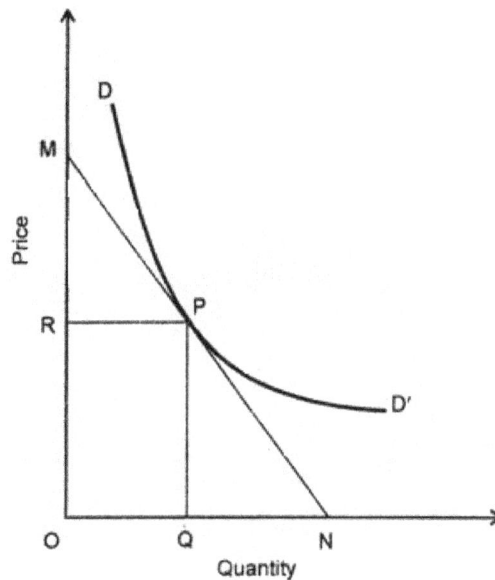

Fig 2.6: Point Elasticity on a non-linear Demand Curve

It follows that at mid-point of a linear demand curve, e = 1, as shown at point P in Fig. 2.6, because both lower and upper segments are equal (i.e., PN = PM) at any other point to the left of point P, e > I and at any point to the right of point.

Price Elasticity at Terminal Points

The price elasticity at terminal point N equals 0 i.e. at point N, e = 0. At terminal point M, however, price-elasticity is undefined, though most texts show that at terminal point M, e = ∞. According to William J. Baumol, a Nobel Prize winner, price elasticity at upper terminal point of the demand curve is undefined. It is undefined because measuring elasticity at terminal point (M) involves division of zero and division by-zero is undefined. In his own words, "Here the elasticity is not even defined because an attempt to evaluate the fraction p/x at that point forces us to commit the sign of dividing by zero. The reader who has forgotten why division by zero is immoral may recall that division is the reverse operation of multiplication. Hence, in seeking the quotient c = a/b we look for a number, c, which when multiplied by b gives us the number a, i.e., for which cb = a. But if a is not zero, say a = 5 and b is zero, there is no such number because there is no c such that c x 0 = 5".

(B) Measuring Arc Elasticity

The concept of point elasticity is pertinent where change in price and the resulting change in quantity are infinite or small. However, where change in price and the consequent hunger in demand is substantial, the concept of arc elasticity is the relevant concept. Arc elasticity is a measure of the average of responsiveness of the quantity demanded to a substantial change in the price. In other words, the measure of price elasticity of demand between two finite points on a demand curve is known as arc activity. For example, the measure of elasticity between points J and K (Fig. 2.7) is: the measure of arc elasticity. The movement from point J to K along the demand curve D) shows a fall in price from Rs 25 to Rs 10 so that AP = 25 - 10 = 15. The consequent increase in demand, AQ = 30 - 50 = - 20. The arc elasticity between point J and K and (moving from J to K) can be obtained by substituting these values in the elasticity formula.

$$e_p = \frac{\Delta Q}{\Delta P} \cdot \frac{P}{Q} \qquad = -\frac{-20}{15} \cdot \frac{25}{30} = 1.11$$

..........eq. I

It means that a one percent decrease in price of commodity X results in a 1.11 percent increase in demand for it.

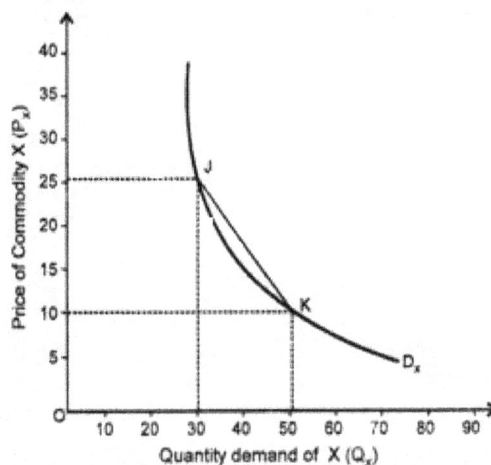

Fig 2.7: Measuring Arc Elasticity

Problems in Using Arc Elasticity

The use of arc elasticity in economic analysis entails a good deal of chariness because it is capable of being misinterpreted. Arc elasticity coefficients differ between the same two finite points on a demand curve if direction of change in price is reversed. Arc elasticity for a decrease in price will be different from that for the same increase in price between the same to points on a demand curve. For example, the price elasticity between points J and K — moving from J to K — is equal to 1.11. This is the elasticity for decrease in price from Rs 25 to Rs 10. But a reverse movement on the demand curve, i.e., from point K to J implies an increase in price from Rs 10 to Rs 25 which will give a different elasticity coefficient. In case of movement from point K to J, P = 10, $\blacktriangle$P = 10 - 25 = - 15, Q = 50 and $\blacktriangle$Q = 50 - 30 = 20. Substituting these values in the elasticity formula, we get

$$e_p = -\frac{20}{-15} \cdot \frac{10}{50} = 0.26$$

The measure of arc elasticity co-efficient in equation I for the reverse movement in price is obviously different from the one given in equation II. Therefore, while measuring the arc elasticity, the direction of price change should be carefully noted, otherwise it may yield misleading conclusions.

A method suggested to resolve this problem is to use the average of upper and lower values of P and Q in fraction, P/Q, so that the formula is

$$e_p = \frac{\Delta Q}{\Delta P} \cdot \frac{(P_1 + P_2)/2}{(Q_1 + Q_2)/2}$$

$$= \frac{Q_1 - Q_2}{P_1 - P_2} \cdot \frac{(P_1 + P_2)/2}{(Q_1 + Q_2)/2}$$

Substituting the values from this example, we get

$$e_p = -\frac{30 - 50}{25 - 10} \cdot \frac{(10 + 25)/2}{(30 + 50)/2} = 0.58$$

This method has its own drawbacks as the elasticity co-efficient calculated through this formula, refers to the elasticity of demand at mid-point between points J and K (Fig. 2.7). Elasticity co-efficient (0.58) is not applicable for the whole range of price-quantity combinations at different points between J and K on the demand curve (Fig. 2.7). It gives only mean of the elasticity between the two points. It is important to note that elasticity between the mid-point and the upper point J or lower point K will be different. Thus, this method does not give one measure of elasticity.

2.4.3 NATURE OF DEMAND CURVES AND ELASTICITY

Generally, elasticity of a demand curve throughout its length is not the same (Fig. 2.8). It varies between 0 and ∞, or in other words,

$$0 \leq e_p \leq \infty$$

In some cases, however, the elasticity remains the same throughout the length of the demand curve. Such demand curves can be placed in the following categories: (i) perfectly inelastic (e = 0); (ii) unitary elastic (e = 1); and (iii) perfectly elastic (e = ∞). These three types of demand curves are illustrated in Fig. 2.8 (a), (b) and (c), respectively.

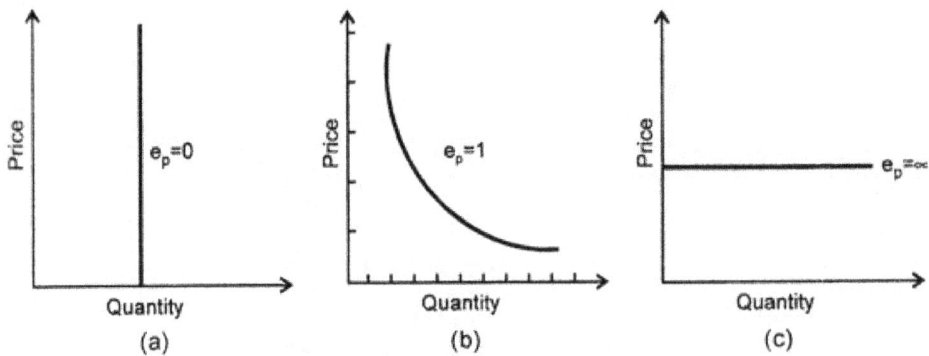

Fig 2.8: Constant Elasticity Demand Curve

2.4.4 SLOPE OF THE DEMAND CURVE AND PRICE ELASTICITY

The elasticity of a demand curve is often judged by its appearance: the flatter the demand curve, the greater the elasticity and vice versa. But this conclusion is misleading because two demand curves with different slopes may have the same elasticity at a given price. In fact, what appearance of a demand curve reveals is its slope, not the elasticity. The slope of the demand curve is the marginal relationship between change in price (▲P) and change in quantity demanded (▲Q). The slope of demand curve is expressed as ▲P/▲Q. It is the reciprocal of the slope ▲Q/▲P which appears in the elasticity formula, not the slope itself.

We will show below: (i) that demand curves having different slopes may have the same elasticity at a given price and (ii) that demand curves having the same slope may have different elasticity at a given price.

(A) ELASTICITY OF DEMAND CURVES HAVING DIFFERENT SLOPES

Let us first illustrate that two demand curves with different slops may have the same elasticity at a given price. In Fig. 2.9, demand curves AB and AD have different slopes. It may be proved as follows:

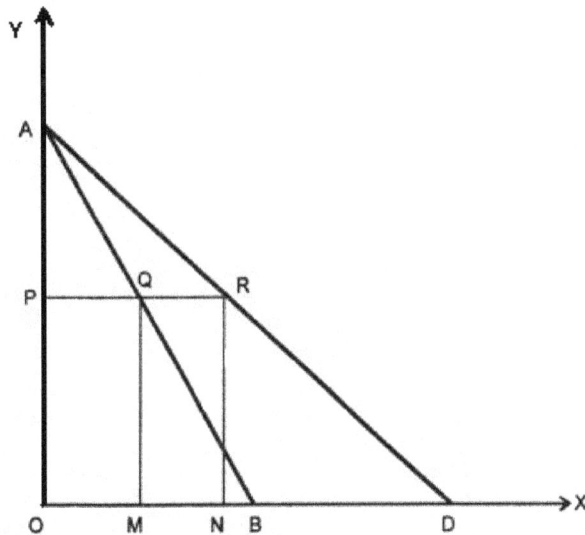

Fig 2.9: Demand Curves having different slopes

Slope of the demand curve AB=OA/OB and

Slope of the demand curve AD=OA/OD

Note that in these ratios, numerator OA is common to both the fractions, but in case of denominators OB<OD.

Therefore, $\dfrac{OA}{OB} < \dfrac{OA}{OD}$

Obviously, the slopes of the two demand curves are different. Let us now show, that at a given price, both the demand curves have the same elasticity. As shown in Fig. at a given price OP, the relevant points for measuring the elasticity are Q and R on the demand curves AB and AD, respectively. Recall that the elasticity at a point on a linear demand curve is obtained as

$$e_p = \frac{\text{Lower segment}}{\text{Upper segment}}$$

Thus, at point Q on demand curve AB, $e_p = QB/QA$ and at point R on AD, $e_p = RD/RA$

Thus, at point Q on demand curve AB, e = QB/QA and at point R on AD, e_p = RD/RA. It can be geometrically proved that the two elasticity are equal, i.e., QB=RD

Let us first consider ▲AOB. If we draw a horizontal line from point Q to intersect the vertical axis at point P and an ordinate from Q to M at the horizontal axis, we have three triangles— ▲AOB, ▲APQ and ▲QMB. Note that ▲AOB, ▲APQ and ▲QMB are right-angles. Therefore, all the three triangles are right-angled triangles. As noted above, the ratios of their two corresponding sides of similar right-angle triangles are always equal. Considering only the relevant triangles, ▲APQ and ▲QMB, we have

$$\frac{BQ}{MQ} = \frac{AQ}{AP}$$

Since MQ = OP, by substituting OP for QM in ratio BQ/MQ, we get

$$\frac{BQ}{OP} = \frac{AQ}{AP}$$

Therefore, $\dfrac{BQ}{AQ} = \dfrac{OP}{AP}$ = Elasticity of demand curve AB, at point Q or at price OP.

We can similarly prove that

$\dfrac{RD}{RA} = \dfrac{OP}{PA}$ = Elasticity of demand curve AD at point R or at price OP.

Thus it is proved, that at price OP,

$$\frac{QB}{QA} = \frac{RD}{RA} = \frac{PO}{PA}$$

It is thus proved that two demand curves with different slopes have the same elasticity at a given price.

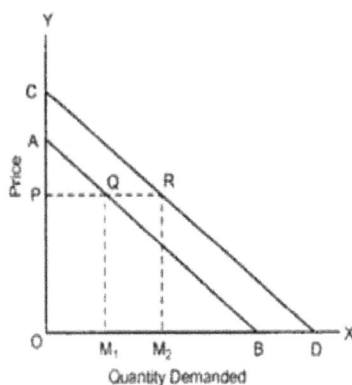

Fig 2.10: Price Elasticity of two parallel demand curves

Now, we will compare the price elasticity at two parallel demand curves at a given price. This has been illustrated in Fig 2.10 where two demand curves AB and CD are given which are parallel to each other. The two demand curves which are parallel to each other imply that they have the same slope. Now, we can prove that at price OP price elasticity of demand on the two demand curves AB and CD is different. Now, draw a perpendicular from point R to the point P on Y-axis. Thus, at price OP the corresponding points on the two demand curves are Q and R respectively.

The elasticity of demand on the demand curve AB at point Q will be equal to QB/QA and at point R on the demand curve CD it is equal to RD/RC.

Because it is right-angled triangle OAB, PQ is parallel to QB:

Therefore, $$\frac{QB}{QA} = \frac{OP}{PA}$$

Hence, price elasticity at point Q on the demand curve

$$AB = \frac{OP}{PA}$$

At point R on the demand curve CD, price elasticity is equal to RD/RC. Because in the right angled triangle OCD, PR is parallel to OD.

Therefore, $$\frac{RD}{RC} = \frac{OP}{PC}$$

Hence, on point R on the demand curve CD, price elasticity =OP/PC

On seeing the diagram it will be clear that at point Q the price elasticity OP/PA and at point R the price elasticity OP/PC are not equal to each other. Because PC is greater than PA,

Managerial Economics   49

$$\frac{OP}{PC} = \frac{OP}{PA}$$

It is therefore; clear that at point R on the demand curve CD the price elasticity is less than that at point Q on the demand curve AB, when the two demand curves being parallel to each other have the same slope. It also follows that as the demand curve shifts to the right the price elasticity of demand at a given price goes on declining. Thus, as has been just seen, price elasticity at price OP on the demand curve CD is less than that on the demand curve AB.

2.4.5 PRICE ELASTICITY AND MARGINAL REVENUE

In this section, we look at one of the most important uses of the price elasticity of demand, used especially in business decision-making. It pertains to the relationship between price elasticity and the marginal change in the total revenue of the firm planning to change the price of its product. The relationship between price elasticity and the marginal revenue (MR) can be derived as follows.

Let us suppose that a given output, Q, is being sold at a price P, so that the total revenue, TR, equals P times Q, i.e.

TR = P X Q ....Eq. I

Since P and Q in eq. I are inversely related, a question arises, whether a change in P will increase or decrease or leave the TR unaffected. It depends on whether MR is greater than or less than or equal to zero, i.e., whether

MR > 0, MR < 0, or MR = 0

The marginal revenue, (MR) can be obtained by differentiating TR = PQ with respect to P as shown below.

$$MR = \frac{\partial(PQ)}{\partial Q}$$

$$= P\frac{\partial Q}{\partial Q} + Q\frac{\partial P}{\partial Q}$$

$$= P + Q\frac{\partial P}{\partial Q}$$

$$MR = P\left(1 + \frac{Q}{P} \cdot \frac{\partial P}{\partial Q}\right)$$

Note that $\frac{Q}{P} \cdot \frac{\partial P}{\partial Q}$ is the reciprocal of the elasticity which equals

$$-\frac{P}{Q} \cdot \frac{\partial Q}{\partial P}$$

Therefore, $\quad \frac{Q}{P} \cdot \frac{\partial P}{\partial Q} = -\frac{1}{e}$

By substituting $-\frac{1}{e}$ for $\frac{Q}{P} , \frac{\partial P}{\partial Q}$ in Eq. I, we get

$$MR = P\left(1 - \frac{1}{e}\right) \quad \text{................Eq. II}$$

Equation II gives the relationship between price-elasticity (e) and MR.

1. Price elasticity and total revenue

Given the relationship between marginal revenue and price elasticity of demand in Eq. II, the decision-makers can easily know whether or not it is advantageous to change the price. Given Eq. II, if e = 1, MR = 0. Therefore, change in price will not cause any change in TR. If e < 1, MR < 0 and, therefore, TR decreases when price decreases and TR increases when price increases. And, if e > 1, MR > 0, then TR increases if price decreases and TR increases when price increases.

The effect of change in price on TR for different price-elasticity co-efficient is summarised in the table mentioned below:

Table 2.3: Elasticity, Price change and change in TR

Elasticity Demand	Nature of Price	Change in TR	Change in co-efficient
$e_p = 0$	Perfectly inelastic	Increase	Increases
		Decrease	Decreases

$e_p < 1$	Inelastic	Increase	Increases
		Decrease	Decreases
$e_p = 1$	Unitary elastic	Increase	No change in TR
		Decrease	
$e_p > 1$	Elastic	Increase	Decrease
		Decrease	Increases
$e_p = \infty$	Infinitely elastic	Increase	Decrease
			Decrease to zero
			Increase infinitely

As the table shows, when e = 0, the demand is said to be perfectly inelastic. Perfect inelasticity of demand implies no change in quantity demanded when price is changed. Therefore, a rise in price will increase the total revenue and vice versa. In case of an inelastic demand (i.e., e < I), quantity demanded increases less than the proportionate decrease in price and hence the total revenue falls when price falls. Total revenue increases when price increases because quantity demanded decreases less than proportionately. If demand for a product is unit-elastic (e = 1) quantity demanded increases (or decreases) in the proportion of decrease (or increase) in the price. Therefore, the total revenue remains unaffected. If demand for a commodity has e > 1, change in quantity demanded is greater than the proportionate change in price. Therefore, the total revenue increases when price falls and vice versa. The case of an infinitely elastic demand is rare. Such a demand line simply implies that a consumer has the opportunity of buying any quantity of a commodity and the seller can sell any quantity of the commodity, at a given price: it is the case of a commodity being bought and sold in a perfectly competitive market.

2.4.6 PRICE ELASTICITY AND CONSUMPTION EXPENDITURE

Another important relationship which is often referred to in economic analysis is the relationship between price elasticity and consumption expenditure. From the law of demand, we know that quantity demanded of a commodity increases when its price falls. But, what happens to the total expenditure on that commodity: does it fall or increase?

The relationship between price-elasticity and total consumption expenditure may be derived as follows. Suppose that the total expenditure, E_x on a commodity X, at a given price,

P, all other prices remaining the same, is given by

$$E_X = Q_X \cdot P_X \ldots \ldots \ldots \ldots \text{Eq. III}$$

By differentiating Eq. III with respect to P_X, we get marginal expenditure (ME), as

$$ME = \frac{\partial E_x}{\partial P_x} = Q_x + \dot{P}_x \frac{\partial Q_x}{\partial P_x}$$

$$= Q_x \left(1 + \frac{P_x}{Q_x} \cdot \frac{\partial Q_x}{\partial P_x} \right)$$

$$\ldots \ldots \ldots \ldots \text{ Eq. IV}$$

In Eq. III , the term $\dfrac{P_x}{Q_x} \cdot \dfrac{\partial Q_x}{\partial P_x}$ gives the price elasticity of consumer expenditure

(e_{ce}) in response to change in price. That is.

$$\frac{P_x}{Q_x} \cdot \frac{\partial Q_x}{\partial P_x} = e_{ce}$$

By substitution, we get

$$ME = \frac{\partial E_x}{\partial P_x}$$

$$= Q_x (1 - e_{ce}) \ldots \ldots \ldots \ldots \text{ Eq.}$$

It may be inferred from Eq. IV that whether the total expenditure increases, decreases or remains constant depends on whether

$$ME \left(= \frac{\partial E_x}{\partial P_x} \right) \gtreqless 0$$

It depends on whether $e_{ce} \gtreqless 1$.

The relationship between, total expenditure and price elasticity of demand has summed up in the following table:

Table 2.4: Elasticity and Consumption Expenditure

Elasticity (e_{ce})	Price change	Marginal Expenditure Expenditure	Total Consumer
$e_{ce} < 1$	Rise	ME < 1	Decreases
	Fall	ME > 1	Increases

$e_{ce} = 1$	Rise	ME = 1	Constant
	Fall	ME = 1	Constant
$e_{ce} > 1$	Rise	ME < 1	Increases
	Fall	ME > 1	Decreases

As shown in Table 2.4, when $e_{ce} > 1$, e.g., demand is elastic, an increase in price causes more than proportionate decrease in quantity demanded. Hence, total expenditure decreases. And, if price decreases quantity demanded increases more than proportionately. As a result, total expenditure increases.

When $e_{ce} = 1$, a rise (or fall) in price causes a proportionate fall (or rise) in quantity demanded leaving total expenditure unchanged.

When $e_{ce} < 1$, i.e., when demand is inelastic, a rise in price causes a rise in the total expenditure because demand decreases less than proportionately and a fall in price reduces it as quantity demanded increases less than proportionately.

2.4.7 CROSS-ELASTICITY OF DEMAND

The cross-elasticity is the measure of responsiveness of demand for a commodity to the changes in the price of its substitutes and complementary goods. For instance, cross-elasticity of demand for tea (T) is the percentage change in its quantity demanded with respect to the change in the price of its substitute, coffee (C). The formula for measuring cross-elasticity of demand for tea ($e_{t,c}$) with respect to price of coffee (P_c)

$$e_{t,c} = \frac{\text{Proportionate change in demand for tea } (Q_t)}{\text{Proportionate change in price of coffee } (P_c)}$$

$$= \frac{P_c}{Q_t} \cdot \frac{\Delta Q_t}{\Delta P_c}$$

The cross elasticity of demand for coffee (QC) with respect to price of tea (Pt) is

$$e_{c,t} = \frac{P_t}{Q_c} \cdot \frac{\Delta Q_c}{\Delta P_t} \quad \text{.......... Eq. V}$$

For example, suppose that price of coffee (P_e) increases from Rs 10 to Rs 15, per 10 grams and as a result demand for tea increases from 20 tons to 30 tons per week, price of tea remaining constant. By substituting these values in Eq. V, we get cross-elasticity of demand for tea with respect to price of coffee, as

$$e_{t,c} = \frac{10}{20} \cdot \frac{20-30}{10-15}$$

$$= \frac{10}{20} \cdot \frac{-10}{-5}$$

$$= 1.0$$

It is important to note that cross-elasticity between any two substitute goods is always positive.

The same formula is used to calculate the cross-elasticity of demand for a good in reaction to the change in the price of its complementary goods. Electricity to electrical gadgets, petrol to automobile, butter to bread, sugar and milk to tea and coffee, are the examples of complementary goods. Notice that the demand for complementary goods has negative cross-elasticity e.g. rise in the price of a good reduces the demand for its complementary goods.

A significant characteristic of cross-elasticity is that if cross-elasticity between two goods is positive, the two may be regarded as substitutes for each other. Moreover, the greater the cross-elasticity, the closer the substitute. Likewise, if cross-elasticity of demand for two related goods is negative, the two may be regarded as complementary of each other: the higher the negative cross-elasticity, the higher the degree of complementarily.

2.4.8 INCOME ELASTICITY OF DEMAND

Aside from the price of a product and its substitutes, another vital element of demand for a product is consumer's income. As noticed previously, the relationship between demand for regular and luxury goods and consumer's income is of positive nature, not like the negative price-demand relationship. I.e, the demand for regular goods and services rises with the rise in consumer's income and vice versa. The reaction of demand to the change in consumer's income is known as income elasticity of demand.

Income elasticity of demand for a product, say X (i.e., e_x) is defined as

$$e_X = \frac{\dfrac{\Delta X}{X}}{\dfrac{\Delta Y}{Y}}$$

Where X = quantity of X demanded; Y = disposable income; ▲X = change in quantity demanded of X; and ▲Y = change in income.

Unlike price elasticity of demand (which is negative except in case of Giffen goods), income elasticity of demand is positive because of a positive relationship between income and demand for a product. There is an exception to this rule. Income elasticity of demand for an inferior good is negative, because of negative income-effect. The demand for inferior goods reduces with the rise in consumer's income and vice versa. When income is more, consumers change over to the consumption of superior commodities. I.e. they replace inferior goods for superior ones. For instance, when income increases, people would rather purchase more of rice and wheat and less of inferior food grains like bajara, ragi and use more of taxi and less of bus service and so on.

NATURE OF COMMODITY AND INCOME ELASTICITY

For all regular goods, income elasticity is positive although the degree of elasticity fluctuates as per the nature of commodities. Consumer goods are usually categorised under three classes, viz. necessities (essential consumer goods), comforts and luxuries. The universal structure of income elasticity for goods of various categories or a rise in income and their effect on sales are provided in Table 2.5. The income elasticity of demand for different categories of goods may still show discrepancies from house to house and from time to time, as per the options, taste and preference of the consumers, degree of their consumption and income and their receptiveness to 'demonstration effect'. The other aspect which could bring about a deviation from the universal structure of income elasticity is the frequency of rise in income. Income rises often and repeatedly, income-elasticity as provided in Table 2.5 follows the universal structure.

A few significant uses of income elasticity are as follows:

First, the concept of income elasticity can be used to approximately calculate the potential demand only if the rate of rise in income and income elasticity of demand for the commodities are identified. The information of income elasticity can hence be useful in predicting demand, when changes in personal incomes are anticipated, other things remaining the same.

Table 2.5: Income Elasticity of different consumer goods

Commodities	Coefficient of income elasticity	Impact on expenditure
Necessities	Less than unitary ($e_y < 1$)	Less than proportionate change in income
Comforts	Almost equal to unity ($e_y = 1$)	Almost proportionate change in income
Luxuries	Greater than unity ($e_y > 1$)	More than proportionate increase in income

Second, the concept of income elasticity could furthermore be used to describe the 'regular' and 'inferior' goods. The goods whose income elasticity is positive for all levels of income are termed as 'regular goods'. On the other hand, the goods for which income elasticity is negative, further than a particular level of income, are termed as 'inferior goods'

Study Notes

Assessment
Write notes on the following: 1.   Elasticity of Demand 2.   Arc Elasticity of Demand 3.   Price Elasticity and Marginal Revenue

4.	Price Elasticity and Consumption Expenditure
5.	Nature of Demand Curves and Elasticity
6.	Cross elasticity and income elasticity.

Discussion

Discuss the problems in using Arc Elasticity.

2.5 Determinants of Demand

Price elasticity of demand fluctuates from commodity to commodity. While the demand of some commodities is highly elastic, the demand for others is highly inelastic. In this section, we will describe the main determinants of the price elasticity of demand.

1. Availability of Substitutes

One of the most significant determinants of elasticity of demand for a commodity is the availability of its substitutes. Closer the substitute, greater is the elasticity of demand for the commodity. For instance, coffee and tea could be regarded as close substitutes for one another. Thus, if price of one of these goods rises, its demand reduces more than the proportionate rise in its price as consumers switch over to the relatively lower-priced substitute. Moreover, broader the choice of the substitutes, greater is the elasticity. E.g. soaps, washing powder, toothpastes, shampoos, etc. are available in several brands; each brand is a close substitute for the other. Thus, the price-elasticity of demand for each brand will be to a large extent greater than the general commodity. In contrast, sugar and salt do not have their close substitute and for this reason their price-elasticity is lower.

2. Nature of Commodity

The nature of a commodity as well has an effect on the price elasticity of its demand. Commodities can be categorised as luxuries, comforts and necessities, on the basis of their nature. Demand for luxury goods (e.g., luxury cars, decorative items, etc.) are more elastic than the demand for other types of goods as consumption of luxury goods can be set aside or delayed when their prices increase. In contrast, consumption of essential goods, (e.g., sugar, clothes, vegetables, etc.) cannot be delayed and for this reason their demand is inelastic. Demand for comforts is usually more elastic than that for necessities and less elastic than the demand for luxuries. Commodities may also be categorised as durable goods and perishable or non-durable goods. Demand for durable goods is more elastic than that for non-durable goods, as when the prices of the former rises, people either get the old one fixed rather than substituting it or buy 'second hand' goods.

3. Proportion of Income Spent on a Commodity

Another aspect that has an impact on the elasticity of demand for a commodity is the proportion of income, which consumers use up on a specific commodity. If proportion of income spent on a commodity is extremely little, its demand will be less elastic and vice versa. Characteristic examples of such commodities are sugar, matches, books, washing powder etc., which use a very tiny proportion of the consumer's income. Demand for these goods is usually inelastic as a rise in the price of such goods does not largely have an effect on the consumer's consumption pattern and the overall purchasing power. Thus, people continue to buy approximately the same quantity even at the time their price rises.

4. Time Factor

Price-elasticity of demand relies moreover on the time which consumers take to amend to a new price: longer the time taken, greater is the elasticity. As each year passes, consumers are capable of altering their spending pattern to price changes. For instance, if the price of bikes falls, demand may not rise instantaneously unless people acquire surplus buying capacity. In the end nevertheless people can alter their spending pattern so that they can purchase a car at a (new) lower price.

5. Range of Alternative Uses of a Commodity

Broader the range of alternative uses of a commodity, higher the price elasticity of its demand intended for the fall in price however less elastic for the increase in price. As the price of a versatile commodity falls, people broaden their consumption to its other uses. Thus, the demand for such a commodity usually rises more than the proportionate fall in its price. E.g., milk can be consumed as it is, it could be transformed into curd, cheese, ghee and buttermilk. The demand for milk will thus be extremely elastic for fall in their price. Likewise, electricity can be utilised for lighting, cooking, heating, as well as for industrial purposes. Thus, demand for electricity is extremely price elastic for fall in its price. For this reason, nevertheless, demand for such goods is inelastic for the increase in their price.

6. The Proportion of Market Supplied

Price elasticity of market demand furthermore relies on the proportion of the market supplied at the determined price. If less than half of the market is supplied at the determined price, elasticity of demand will be higher if more than half of the market is supplied. i.e. demand curve is more elastic at the upper half than at the lower half.

🔔	**Study Notes**

👁	**Assessment**

What are the factors, which determine the demand of a commodity? Explain.

🗣	**Discussion**

Discuss how availability of Substitute goods determines the demand of a good.

2.6   Demand Forecasting

Demand forecasting entails forecasting and estimating the quantity of a product or service that consumers will purchase in future. It tries to evaluate the magnitude and significance of forces that will affect future operating conditions in an enterprise. Demand forecasting involves use of various formal and informal forecast techniques such as informed guesses, use of historical sales data or current field data gathered from representative markets. Demand forecasting may be used in making pricing decisions, in assessing future capacity requirements, or in making decisions on whether to enter a new market. Thus, demand forecasting is estimation of future demand. According to Cardiff and Still, "Demand forecasting is an estimate of sales during a specified future period based on a proposed marketing plan and a set of particular uncontrollable and competitive forces". As such, demand forecasting is a projection of firm's expected future demands.

2.6.1 DEMAND FORECAST AND SALES FORECAST

Due to the dynamic and complex nature of marketing phenomenon, demand forecasting has become an important and regular business exercise. It is essential for profit maximisation and the survival and expansion of a business. However, before selecting any vendor a retailer should well understand the requirement and the importance of demand forecasting. In management circles, demand forecasting and sales forecasting are used interchangeably. Sales forecasts are first approximations in production and forward planning. These provide a platform upon which plans could be prepared and amendments may be made. According to American Marketing Association, "Sales forecast is an estimate of sales in monetary or physical units for a specified future period under a proposed business plan or programmer or under an assumed set of 'economic and other environment forces, planning premises, outside business/ antiquate which the forecast or-estimate is made".

2.6.2 COMPONENTS OF DEMAND FORECASTING SYSTEM

- Market research operations to procure relevant and reliable information about the trends in market.

- A data processing and analysing system to estimate and evaluate the sales performance in various markets.

- Proper co-ordination of steps (i) and (ii) above

- Placing the findings before the top management for making final decisions.

2.6.3 OBJECTIVES OF DEMAND FORECAST

1. Short Term Objectives

a. **Drafting of Production Policy:** Demand forecasts facilitate in drafting appropriate production policy so that there may not be any space between future demand and supply of a product. This can in addition ensure:

- **Routine Supply of Materials:** Demand forecasting assists in figuring out the preferred volume of production. The essential prerequisite of raw materials in future can be calculated on the basis of such forecasts. This guarantees regular and continuous supply of the materials in addition to managing the amount of supply at the economic level.

- **Best Possible Use of Machines:** Demand forecasting in addition expedites cutting down inactive capacity because only the necessary amount of machines and equipments are set up to meet future demands.

- **Regular Availability of Labour:** As soon as demand forecasts are made, supplies of the necessary amount of skilled and unskilled workers can be organised well beforehand to meet the future production plans.

b. **Drafting of Price Policy:** Demand forecasts facilitate the management to prepare a few suitable pricing systems, so that the level of price does not rise and fall to a great extent during depression or inflation.

c. **Appropriate Management of Sales**: Demand forecasts are made area wise and after that the sales targets for different regions are set in view of that. This abets the calculation of sales performances.

d. **Organising Funds**: On the basis of demand forecast, an individual can find out the monetary requirements of the organisation in order to bring about the desired output. This can make it possible to cut down on the expenditure of acquiring funds.

2. **Long Term Goals:** If the demand forecast period is more than a year, in that case it is termed as long term forecast. The following are the key goals of such forecasts:

a. **To settle on the production capacity:** Long term decisions are entwined with capacity variations by adding or discarding capacity in the form of capital assets - manufacturing plants, new technology implementation etc. Size of the organisation should such that output matches with the sales requirements. Organisations that are extremely small or large in size might not be in the financial interest of the company. Inadequate capability can hasten declining delivery performance, needless rise in work-in-process and disturb sales personnel and those in the production unit. Nevertheless, surplus capacity can be expensive and pointless. The incompetence to appropriately deal with capacity can be an obstacle to attaining the best possible performance. By examining the demand pattern for the product as well as the forecasts for the future, the company can prepare for a company's output of the desired capacity.

b. **Labour Requirements:** Spending on labour is one of the most vital elements of cost of production. Dependable and correct demand forecasts can facilitate the management to evaluate suitable labour requirements. This can ensure finest labour supply and uninterrupted production procedures.

c. **Production Planning:** Long term production planning can aid the management in organising long term finances on practical terms and conditions.

The study of long term sales is accorded greater importance as compared with short-term sales. Long term sales forecast facilitates the management to take a few policy decisions of huge importance and any mistake carried out in this could be extremely different or costly to be corrected.

Therefore, the complete success of an organisation usually is contingent upon the quality and authenticity of sales forecasting methods.

2.6.4 IMPORTANCE OF DEMAND FORECAST

1. **Management Decisions:** An effective demand forecast facilitates the management to take appropriate steps in factors that are pertinent to decision making such as plant capacity, raw-material requisites, space and building requirements and availability of labour and capital. Manufacturing schedules can be drafted in compliance with the demand requisites; in this manner cutting down on the inventory, production and other related costs.

2. **Evaluation:** Demand forecasting furthermore smoothes the process of evaluating the efficiency of the sales department.

3. **Quality and Quantity Controls:** Demand forecasting is an essential and valuable instrument in the control of the management of an organisation to provide finished goods of correct quality and quantity at the correct time with the least amount of expenditure.

4. **Financial Estimates:** As per the sales level as well as production functions, the financial requirements of an organisation can be calculated using various techniques of demand forecasting. In addition, it needs a little time to acquire revenue on practical terms. Sales forecasts will, as a result, make it possible for arranging adequate resources on practical terms and in advance as well.

5. **Avoiding Surplus and Inadequate Production:** Demand forecasting is necessary for the old and new organisations. It is somewhat essential if an organisation is engaged in large scale production of goods and the development period is extremely time-consuming in the course of production. In such situations, an estimate regarding the future demand is essential to avoid inadequate and surplus production.

6. **Recommendations for the future:** Demand forecast for a specific commodity furthermore provides recommendations for demand forecast of associated industries.

E.g. the demand forecast for the vehicle industry aids the tyre industry in calculating the demand for two wheelers, three wheelers and four wheelers.

7. **Significance for the government:** At the macro-level, demand forecasting is valuable to the government as it aids in determining targets of imports as well as exports for various products and preparing for the international business.

2.6.5 METHODS OF DEMAND FORECAST

No demand forecasting method is 100% precise. Collective forecasts develop precision and decrease the probability of huge mistakes.

1. **Methods that relay on Qualitative Assessment:**

   Forecasting demand based on expert opinion. Some of the types in this method are:

   - Unaided judgment

   - Prediction market

   - Delphi technique

   - Game theory

   - Judgmental bootstrapping

   - Simulated interaction

   - Intentions and expectations surveys

   - Conjoint analysis

2. **Methods that rely on quantitative data:**

   - Discrete event simulation

   - Extrapolation

   - Quantitative analogies

   - Rule-based forecasting

   - Neural networks

   - Data mining

   - Causal models

   - Segmentation

1. **Prediction markets:** These are speculative markets fashioned with the intention of making predictions. Assets that are produced possess an ultimate cash worth bound to a specific event (e.g. who will win the next election) or situation (e.g., total sales next quarter). The present market prices can then be described as forecasts of the likelihood of the event or the estimated value of the situation. Prediction markets are as a result planned as betting exchanges, without any kind of compromise for the bookmaker. People who buy low and sell high are rewarded for improving the market prediction, while those who buy high and sell low are punished for degrading the market prediction. Evidence so far suggests that prediction markets are at least as accurate as other institutions predicting the same events with a similar pool of participants.

   Many prediction markets are open to the public. Betfair is the world's biggest prediction exchange, with around $28 billion traded in 2007. Intrade is a for-profit company with a large variety of contracts not including sports. The Iowa Electronic Markets is an academic market examining elections where positions are limited to $500. Trade Sports are prediction markets for sporting events.

2. **Delphi method:** This is a systematic, interactive forecasting method which relies on a panel of experts. The experts answer questionnaires in two or more rounds. After each round, a facilitator provides an anonymous summary of the experts' forecasts from the previous round as well as the reasons they provided for their judgments. Thus, experts are encouraged to revise their earlier answers in light of the replies of other members of their panel. It is believed that during this process the range of the answers will decrease and the group will converge towards the 'correct' answer. Finally, the process is stopped after a pre-defined stop criterion (e.g. number of rounds, achievement of consensus, stability of results) and the mean or median scores of the final rounds determine the results.

3. **Game theory:** Game theory is a branch of applied mathematics that is used in the social sciences, most notably in economics, as well as in biology (particularly evolutionary biology and ecology), engineering, political science, international relations, computer science and philosophy. Game theory attempts at mathematically capturing behaviour in strategic situations or games in which an individual's success in making choices depends on the choices of others. While initially developed to analyse competitions in which one individual does better at another's expense (zero sum games), it has been expanded to

treat a wide class of interactions, which are classified according to several criteria. Today, "game theory is a sort of umbrella or 'unified field' theory for the rational side of social science, where 'social' is interpreted broadly, to include human as well as non-human players (computers, animals, plants)" (Aumann 1987).

Traditional applications of game theory aim at finding equilibrium in these games. In equilibrium, each player of the game has adopted a strategy that they are unlikely to change. Many equilibrium concepts have been developed (most famously the Nash equilibrium) in an endeavor to capture this idea. These equilibrium concepts are differently motivated depending on the field of application, although they often overlap or coincide. This methodology is not without criticism and debates continue over the appropriateness of particular equilibrium concepts, the appropriateness of equilibrium altogether and the usefulness of mathematical models more generally.

Although, some developments occurred before it, the field of game theory came into being with Émile Borel's researches in his 1938 book *Applications aux Jeux des Hazard* and was followed by the 1944 book *Theory of Games and Economic Behavior* by John von Neumann and Oskar Morgenstern. This theory was developed extensively in the 1950s by many scholars. Game theory was later explicitly applied to biology in the 1970s, although similar developments go back at least as far as the 1930s. Game theory has been widely recognised as an important tool in many fields. Eight game theorists have won the Nobel Memorial Prize in Economic Sciences and John Maynard Smith was awarded the Crafoord Prize for his application of game theory to biology.

The games studied in game theory are well-defined mathematical objects. A game consists of a set of players, a set of moves (or strategies) available to those players and a specification of payoffs for each combination of strategies. Most cooperative games are presented in the characteristic function form, while the extensive and the normal forms are used to define non-cooperative games.

QUANTITATIVE DATA

1. **Discrete-event simulation:** The operation of a system is represented as a chronological sequence of events. Each event occurs at an instant in time and marks a change of state in the system. For example, if an elevator is simulated, an event could be "level 6 button pressed", with the resulting system state of "lift moving" and eventually (unless one chooses to simulate the failure of the lift) "lift at level 6".

A common exercise in learning how to build discrete-event simulations is to model a queue, such as customers arriving at a bank to be served by a teller. In this example, the system entities are CUSTOMER-QUEUE and TELLERS. The system events are CUSTOMER-ARRIVAL and CUSTOMER-DEPARTURE. (The event of TELLER-BEGINS-SERVICE can be part of the logic of the arrival and departure events.) The system states, which are changed by these events, are NUMBER-OF-CUSTOMERS-IN-THE-QUEUE (an integer from 0 to n) and TELLER-STATUS (busy or idle). The random variables that need to be characterised to model this system stochastically are CUSTOMER-INTERARRIVAL-TIME and TELLER-SERVICE-TIME.

2. **Rule based forecasting:** Rule-based forecasting (RBF) is a proficient method that incorporates judgment as well as statistical techniques to merge forecasts. It involves condition-action statements (rules) where conditions are based on the aspects of the past progress and upon knowledge of that specific area. These rules give in to the load suitable to the forecasting condition as described by the circumstances. In fact, RBF uses structured judgment as well as statistical analysis to modify predictive techniques to the condition. Practical outcomes on several sets of the past progress indicate that RBF generates forecasts that are more precise than those generated by the conventional predictive techniques or by an equal-load amalgamation of predictions.

3. **Data mining:** Data mining is the process of extracting patterns from data. Data mining is seen as an increasingly important tool by modern business to transform data into an informational advantage. It is currently used in a wide range of profiling practices, such as marketing, surveillance and scientific discovery.

   Data mining commonly involves four classes of tasks:

- Clustering - is the task of discovering groups and structures in the data that are in some way or another "similar", without using known structures in the data.

- Classification - is the task of generalising known structure to apply to new data. For example, an email program might attempt to classify an email as legitimate or spam. Common algorithms include decision tree learning, nearest neighbor, naive Bayesian classification, neural networks and support vector machines.

- Regression - Attempts to find a function which models the data with the least error.

- Association rule learning - Searches for relationships between variables. For example a supermarket might gather data on customer purchasing habits. Using association rule learning, the supermarket can determine which products are frequently bought together and use this information for marketing purposes. This is sometimes referred to as market basket analysis.

1. **Regression analysis:** Regression analysis is the statistical technique that identifies the relationship between two or more quantitative variables: a dependent variable whose value is to be predicted and an independent or explanatory variable (or variables), about which knowledge is available. The technique is used to find the equation that represents the relationship between the variables. A simple regression analysis can show that the relation between an independent variable X and a dependent variable Y is linear, using the simple linear regression equation Y= a + bX (where a and b are constants). Multiple regression will provide an equation that predicts one variable from two or more independent variables, $Y = a + bX_1 + cX_2 + dX_3$.

The steps in regression analysis are:

   a. **Construction of the causal model:** The construction of an explanatory model is a crucial step in the regression analysis. It must be defined with reference to the action theory of the intervention. It is likely that several kinds of variable exist. In some cases, they may be specially created, for example to take account of the fact that an individual has benefited from support or not (a dummy variable, taking values 0 or 1). A variable may also represent an observable characteristic (having a job or not) or an unobservable one (probability of having a job). The model may presume that a particular variable evolves in a linear, logarithmic, exponential or other way. All the explanatory models are constructed on the basis of a model, such as the following, for linear regression:

   $Y = \beta_0 + \beta_1 X_1 + \beta_2 X_2 + ... + \beta_k X_k + \varepsilon$, where

   Y is the change that the programme is mainly supposed to produce (e.g. employment of trainees)

   X_{1-k} are independent variables likely to explain the change.

   β_{0-k} are constants and

   ε is the error term

   Phenomena of co-linearity weaken the explanatory power. For example, when questioning women about unemployment, if they have experienced periods of previous unemployment which are systematically longer than those of men, it will not be possible to separate the influence of the two explanatory factors: gender and duration of previous unemployment.

b. **Construction of a sample:** To apply multiple regression, a large sample is usually required (ideally between 2,000 to 15,000 individuals). Note that for time series data, much less is needed.

c. **Data collection:** Reliable data must be collected, either from a monitoring system, from a questionnaire survey or from a combination of both.

d. **Calculation of coefficients:** Coefficients can be calculated relatively easily, using statistical software that is both affordable and accessible to PC users.

e. **Test of the model:** The model aims to explain as much of the variability of the observed changes as possible. To check how useful a linear regression equation is, tests can be performed on the square of the correlation coefficient r. This tells us what percentage of the variability in the y variable can be explained by the x variable. A correlation coefficient of 0.9 would show that 81% of the variability in Y is captured by the variables X_{1-k} used in the equation. The part that remains unexplained represents the residue (ε). Thus, the smaller the residue better is the quality of the model and its adjustment. The analysis of residues is a very important step: it is at this stage that one sees the degree to which the model has been adapted to the phenomena one wants to explain. It is the residue analysis that also enables one to tell whether the tool has made it possible to estimate the effects in a plausible way or not. If significant anomalies are detected, the regression model should not be used to estimate effects and the original causal model should be re-examined, to see if further predictive variables can be introduced.

2. **Time series analysis:** An analysis of the relationship between variables over a period of time. Time-series analysis is useful in assessing how an economic or other variable changes over time. For example, one may conduct a time-series analysis on a stock, sales volumes, interest rates and quality measurements etc.

    Methods for time series analyses may be divided into two classes: frequency-domain methods (spectral analysis and recently wavelet analysis) and time-domain methods (auto-correlation and cross-correlation).

a. **Frequency domain:** Frequency domain is a term used to describe the domain for analysis of mathematical functions or signals with respect to frequency, rather than time. A time-domain graph shows how a signal changes over time. Whereas a frequency-domain graph shows how much of the signal lies within each given frequency band over a range of frequencies. A frequency-domain representation can also include information on the phase shift that must be applied to each sinusoid in order to be able to recombine the frequency components to recover the original time signal.

    b. Time domain: Time domain is a term used to describe the analysis of mathematical functions, or physical signals, with respect to time. In the time domain, the signal or function's value is known for all real numbers, for the case of continuous time, or at various separate instants in the case of discrete time. An oscilloscope is a tool commonly used to visualise real-world signals in the time domain.

3. **Utility analysis:** A subset of consumer demand theory that analysis consumer behavior and market demand using total utility and marginal utility. The key principle of utility analysis is the law of diminishing marginal utility, which offers an explanation for the law of demand and the negative slope of the demand curve. The main focus of utility analysis is on the fulfillment of wants and needs acquired by the utilization of goods. It additionally facilitates in getting the knowledge of market demand as well as the law of demand. The law of demand by way of utility analysis states that consumers buy goods that fulfill their wants and needs, i.e., create utility. Those goods that create more utility are more important to consumers and therefore buyers are prepared to pay a higher price. The main aspect to the law of demand is that the utility created falls when the quantity consumed rises. As such, the demand price that buyers are prepared to pay falls when the quantity demanded rises.

    The law of diminishing marginal utility asserts that marginal utility or the extra utility acquired from consuming a good, falls as the quantity consumed rises. Basically, each extra good consumed is less fulfilling as compared to the previous one. This law is mostly significant for awareness into market demand as well as the law of demand.

    a. Cardinal utility: A measure of utility, or satisfaction derived from the consumption of goods and services that can be measured using an absolute scale. Cardinal utility exists if the utility derived from consumption is measurable in the same way that other physical characteristics--height and weight--are measured using a scale that is comparable between people. There is little or no evidence to suggest that such measurement is possible and is not even needed for modern consumer demand theory and indifference curve analysis. Cardinal utility, however, is often employed as a convenient teaching device for discussing such concepts as marginal utility and utility maximisation.

b. **Ordinal utility:** A method of analysing utility, or satisfaction derived from the consumption of goods and services, based on a relative ranking of the goods and services consumed. With ordinal utility, goods are only ranked only in terms of more or less preferred, there is no attempt to determine how much more one good is preferred to another. Ordinal utility is the underlying assumption used in the analysis of indifference curves and should be compared with cardinal utility, which (hypothetically) measures utility using a quantitative scale.

	Study Notes

	Assessment

Write notes on the following:

1. Objectives of Demand Forecast

2. Importance of Demand Forecast

3. Methods of Demand Forecast

4. Regression analysis

5. Cardinal utility

6. Ordinal utility

🗣	**Discussion**

Discuss Delphi method and Game theory in detail.

2.7 Summary

Demand: "The demand for a commodity at a given price is the amount of it which will be bought per unit of time at that price".

Law of Demand: "The demand for a commodity increases with a fall in its price and decreases with a rise in its price, other things remaining the same". The Law of demand thus merely states that the price and demand of a commodity are inversely related, provided all other things remain unchanged or as economists put it ceteris paribus.

Assumptions to the Law of Demand: We can state the assumptions of the law of demand as follows: (1) Income level should remain constant, (2) Tastes of the buyer should not change, (3) Prices of other goods should remain constant, (4) No new substitutes for the commodity, (5) Price rise in future should not be expected and (6) Advertising expenditure should remain the same.

Why Demand Curve Slopes Downwards: The reasons behind the law of demand, i.e., inverse relationship between price and quantity demanded are following: (i) substitution effect, (ii) income effect, (iii) diminishing marginal utility.

Market Demand: The total quantity which all the consumers of a commodity are willing to buy at a given price per time unit, other things remaining the same, is known as market demand for the commodity. In other words, the market demand for a commodity is the sum of individual demands by all the consumers (or buyers) of the commodity, per time unit and at a given price, other factors remaining the same.

Individual demand: The individual demand means the quantity of a product that an individual can buy given its price. It implies that the individual has the ability and willingness to pay.

Demand Function: Demand function is a mathematical expression of the law of demand in quantitative terms. A demand function may produce a linear or curvilinear demand curve depending on the nature of relationship between the price and quantity demanded. The functional relationship between the demand for a commodity and its various determinants may be expressed mathematically as:

Dx = f (Px, Py, M, T, A, U) where, Dx = Quantity demanded for commodity X, f = functional relation, Px = The price of commodity X, Py = The price of substitutes and complementary goods, M = The money income of the consumer, T = The taste of the consumer, A = The advertisement effects, U = Unknown variables or influences

Elasticity of Demand: The concept of elasticity of demand can be defined as the degree of responsiveness of demand to given change in price of the commodity.

Methods of Measurement of Elasticity of Demand: By using three different methods, elasticity of demand is measured.

- Ratio Method

- Expenditure Method

- Point Method

Demand Forecasting: According to Cardiff and Still, "Demand forecasting is an estimate of sales during a specified future period based on a proposed marketing plan and a set of particular uncontrollable and competitive forces".

Objectives of Demand Forecast: Following are the objectives of demand forecasting:

- Formulation of production policy

- Price policy formulation

- Proper control of sales

- Arrangement of finance

- To decide about the production capacity

- Labour requirements

- Production planning

GAME THEORY

Game theory is a branch of applied mathematics that is used in the social sciences, most notably in economics, as well as in biology (particularly evolutionary biology and ecology), engineering, political science, international relations, computer science and philosophy. It attempts to capture behaviour mathematically in strategic situations or games in which an individual's success in making choices depends on the choices of others.

While initially developed to analyse competitions in which one individual does better at another's expense (zero sum games), it has been expanded to include a wide class of interactions, which are classified according to several criteria.

2.8 Self Assessment Test

Broad Questions

1. State the law of demand and show it through a demand schedule and a demand curve. What are the exceptions to the law of demand?

2. Explain the concepts of arc and point elasticity of the demand curve for a commodity. What is the problem in using the arc elasticity? How can this problem be resolved? How is the point elasticity on curvilinear demand curve measured?

3. Prove the following:

   a. Two parallel straight-line demand curves have different price elasticity at the same price.

   b. Two intersecting straight-line demand curves have different elasticity at the point of intersection.

Short Questions

   a. Demand Forecasting

   b. Law of Demand

   c. Increase and decrease in demand

   d. Importance of Demand Forecasting

   e. Methods of measuring Elasticity of Demand

   f. Demand Forecast and Sales Forecast

   g. Prediction markets

   h. Delphi method

   i. Game theory

   j. Regression analysis

   k. Time series analysis

   l. Cardinal utility

   m. Ordinal utility

Numerical Questions:

1. Derive a demand curve from the demand function Q = 50 - 10P.

2. From the demand function Q = 600/P, show that the total expenditure on the commodity remains unchanged as price falls. Estimate elasticity of demand along the demand curve at P = Rs 4 and P = Rs 2.

3. Suppose a demand schedule is given as follows:

Price (Rs)	100	80	60	40	20	0
Quantity	100	200	300	400	500	600

   a. Work out the elasticity for the fall in price from Rs 80 to Rs 60.

   b. Calculate the elasticity for the increase in the price from Rs 60 to Rs 80.

   Why is the elasticity coefficient in (a) different form that in (b)?

2.9 Further Reading

1. Business Economics, Adhikary, M,.., Excel Books, New Delhi, 2000

2. Economics Theory and Operations Analysis, Baumol, W J., 3rd ed., Prentice Hall Inc, 1996

3. Managerial Economics, Chopra, O P., Tata McGraw Hill, New Delhi, 1985

4. Managerial Economics, Keat, Paul G and Philips K Y Young, Prentice Hall, New Jersey, 1996

5. A Modern Micro Economics, Koutsoyiannis, Macmillan, 1991

6. Economics Organisation and Management, Milgrom, P and Roberts J, Prentice Hall Inc, Englewood Clitts, New Jersey, 1992

7. Managerial Economics, Maheshwari, Yogesh, Sultanchand and Sons, 2009

8. Managerial Economics, Varshney, R L., Sultanchand and Sons, 2007

Assignment

1. Which of the following statements are right or wrong?

    a. When percentage change in price is greater than the percentage change in quantity demanded, e > 1

    b. The coefficient of the price-elasticity of a demand curve between any two points remains the same irrespective of whether price falls or rises.

    c. The slope of a demand curve gives the measure of its elasticity.

    d. The slope of demand curve multiplied by P/Q measures the elasticity of demand.

    e. Two parallel straight-line demand curves have the same elasticity at a given price.

    f. Two intersecting straight-line demand curves have the same elasticity at the point of their intersection.

    g. Two straight line demand curves originating at the same point on the price axis have the same elasticity at a given price,

    h. When income increases, the expenditure on essential goods increases more than proportionately

    i. The demand for a product increases when price of its substitute increases,

    j. The greater the cross elasticity, the closer the substitute,

    k. The price elasticity of the supply of a commodity is always negative.

    l. The income elasticity of the demand for luxury goods is always positive,

    m. If price elasticity is less than one and price rises, the total expenditure decreases,

    n. If price elasticity is equal to one, the total revenue increases with the increase in price

    [Ans. Right Statements—(g), (i), (j), (k)]

2. Which of the following gives the measures of price elasticity of demand?

    a. The ratio of change in demand to the change in price

    b. The ratio of change in price to the change in demand

    c. The ratio of % change in demand to % change in price

    d. None of the above

3. Which of the following gives the measure of price elasticity of demand?

   a. (AQ/AP)(P/Q)

   b. (AP/AQHP/Q)

   c. (AQ/AP) (Q/P)

4. Price of a commodity falls and its demand increases so that elasticity is estimated to be 1.25. Suppose price increases back to its old level. Will price elasticity be (a) the same (b) less than 1.25 (c) higher than 1.25?

5. At a given price, two parallel demand curves have

   a. The same point elasticity

   b. Different point elasticity

6. Two intersecting demand curves have at the point of their intersection (a) the same elasticity (b) a different elasticity

7. A less-than-zero income elasticity indicates that with an increase in income, consumption of a product

   (a) Turns negative (b) increase

   (b) Decrease (d) remains constant?

   [Ans. 2. (a), 3. (c), 4. (b), 5. (b), 6. (b), 7. (c)]

_____

_____

_____

_____

_____

_____

_____

_____

_____

_____

_____

_____

Unit 3   Production and Cost Functions

◎	**Learning Outcome**

After going through this unit, you will be able to:

- Discuss Production Function

- Outline Concepts of Cost Functions

- Summarise Concept of isoquants and isocosts

- Explain concepts of Economies and Diseconomies of scale

- Describe Short and Long run Production Function

- Compare Short and Long run Cost Function

🕐	**Time Required to Complete the unit**

1.   1st Reading: It will need 3 Hrs for reading a unit

2.   2nd Reading with understanding: It will need 4 Hrs for reading and understanding a unit

3.   Self Assessment: It will need 3 Hrs for reading and understanding a unit

4.   Assignment: It will need 2 Hrs for completing an assignment

5.   Revision and Further Reading: It is a continuous process

📄	**Content Map**

3.1   **Introduction**

3.2   **Production Function**

      3.2.1   Uses of Production Function

      3.2.2   Types of Production Function

      3.2.3   Short run and Long run Production Function

3.3   Cost Function

    3.3.1   Short run Cost Function

    3.3.2   Relation between AC and MC

    3.3.3   Long run Cost Function

3.4   Production ISOQUANT

    3.4.1   Isoquants

    3.4.2   Types of Isoquants

    3.4.3   Properties of Isoquants

3.5   ISOCOST

3.6   Economies of Scale

    3.6.1   Concept of Economies of Scale

    3.6.2   Laws of Returns to Scale

    3.6.3   Economies and Diseconomies of Scale

3.7   Summary

3.8   Self Assessment Test

3.9   Further Reading

3.1 Introduction

Production functions and cost functions are the cornerstones of business and managerial economics. A production function is a mathematical relationship that captures the essential features of the technology by means of which an organisation metamorphoses resources such as land, labour and capital into goods or services such as steel or cement. It is the economist's distillation of the salient information contained in the engineer's blueprints. Mathematically, let Y denote the quantity of a single output produced by the quantities of inputs denoted $(x_1,..., x_n)$. Then the production function $f(x_1,...,x_n)$ describes how a given output can be produced by an infinite combinations of inputs $(x_1,.., x_n)$, given the technology in use. Several important features of the structure of the technology are captured by the shape of the production function. Relationships among inputs include the degree of substitutability or complementarily among pairs of inputs, as well as the ability to aggregate groups of inputs into a shorter list of input aggregates. Relationships between output and the inputs include economies of scale and the technical efficiency with which inputs are utilised to produce a given output.

Each of these features has implications for the shape of the cost function, which is intimately related to the production function. A cost function is also a mathematical relationship, one that relates the expenses an organisation incurs on the quantity of output it produces and to the unit prices it pays. Mathematically, let E denote the expense an organisation incurs in the production of output quantity Y when it pays unit prices $(p_1,..., p_n)$ for the inputs it employs. Then the cost function $C(y, p_1, ..., p_n)$ describes the minimum expenditure required to produce output quantity Y when input unit prices are $(p_1,..., p_n)$, given the technology in use and so $E \geq C(y, p_1,...,p_n)$. A cost function is an increasing function of $(y, p_1,..., p_n)$, but the degrees to which minimum cost increases with an increase in the quantity of output produced or in any input price depends on the features describing the structure of production technology. For example, scale economies enable output to expand faster than input usage. In other words, proportionate increase in output is larger than the proportionate increase in inputs. Such a situation is also denoted as elasticity of production in relation to inputs being grater than one scale economies thus create an incentive for large-scale production and by analogous reasoning scale diseconomies create a technological deterrent to large-scale production. For another example, if a pair of inputs is a close substitute and the unit price of one of the inputs increases, the resulting increase in cost is less than if the two inputs were poor substitutes or complements. Finally, if wastage in the organisation causes actual output to fall short of maximum possible output or if inputs are misallocated in light of their respective unit prices, then actual cost exceeds minimum cost; both technical and allocative inefficiency are costly.

As these examples suggest, under fairly general conditions the shape of the cost function is a mirror image of the shape of the production function. Thus, the cost function and the production function generally afford equivalent information concerning the structure of production technology. This equivalence relationship between production functions and cost functions is known as 'duality' and it states that one of the two functions has certain features if and only if, the other has certain features. Such a duality relationship has a number of important implications. Since the production function and the cost function are based on different data, duality enables us to employ either function as the basis of an economic analysis of production, without fear of obtaining conflicting inferences. The theoretical properties of associated output supply and input demand equations may be inferred from either the theoretical properties of the production function or, more easily, for those of the dual cost function.

Empirical analysis aimed at investigating the nature of scale economies, the degree of input substitutability or complementarily, or the extent and nature of productive inefficiency can be conducted using a production function or again more easily using a cost function.

If the time period under consideration is sufficiently short, then the assumption of a given technology is valid. The longer-term effects of technological progress or the adaptation of existing superior technology can be introduced into the analysis. Technical progress increases the maximum output that can be obtained from a given collection of inputs and so in the presence of unchanging unit prices of the inputs technical progress reduces the minimum cost that must be incurred to produce a given quantity of output. This phenomenon is merely an extension to the time dimension of the duality relationship that links production functions and cost functions. Of particular empirical interest are the magnitude of technical progress and its cost-reducing effects and the possible labour-saving bias of technological progress and its employment effects that are transmitted from the production function, to the cost function and then to the labour demand function.

3.2 Production Function

Synonymous to the demand theory that pivots around the concept of the demand function, the theory of production revolves around the concept of the production function. A production function can be an equation, table or graph presenting the maximum amount of a commodity that a firm can produce from a given set of inputs during a period of time.

The concept of production function portrays the ways in which the factors of production are combined by a firm to produce different levels of output. More specifically, it shows the maximum volume of physical output available from a given set of inputs or the minimum set of inputs necessary to produce any given level of output.

The production function comprises an engineering or technical relation, because the relation between inputs and outputs is a technical one. The production function is determined by a given state of technology. When the technology improves the production function changes, because the new production function can yield greater output from the given inputs or smaller inputs will be enough to produce a given level of output. Further, the production function incorporates the idea of efficiency. Thus, production function is not any relation between inputs and outputs, but a relation in which a given set of inputs produces a maximum output. Therefore, the production function includes all the technically efficient methods of producing an output.

A method or process of production is a combination of inputs required for the production of output. A method of production is technically efficient to any other method if it uses less of at least one factor and no more of the other factors as compared with another method.

Example: Technically Efficient Method of Production

Let us suppose that commodity X is produced by two methods by using labour and capital:

Factor inputs	Method A	Method B
Labour	3	4
Capital	4	4

In the above example, method B is inefficient compared to method A because method B uses more of labour and same amount of capital as compared to method A. A profit maximising firm will not be interested in improvident or inefficient methods of production. If method A uses less of one factor and more of the other factor as compared with any other method C, then method A and C are not directly comparable. For example, let us suppose that a commodity is produced by two methods:

Factor inputs	Method A	Method C
Labour	3	2
Capital	4	5

In the above example, both methods A and C are technically efficient and are included in the production function, which one of them would be chosen depends on the prices of factors. The choice of any particular technique from a set of technically efficient techniques (or methods) is an economic one, based on prices and not a technical one.

In a production function, the dependent variable is the output and the independent variables are the inputs. Thus, the production function can be expressed as

$Q = f (N,L,K,E,T)$

Where, Q = Quantity Produced, N = Natural resources, L = Labour, K = Capital, E = Entrepreneur or organizer and T = Technology.

For simplicity, only the inputs of labour and capital are considered independent variables in a production function. Normally, land does not enter the production function explicitly because of the implicit assumption that land does not impose any restriction on production. However, labour and capital enter production explicitly. A simple specification of a production function is

$Q = f (L, K)$

Where Q, as above, is the output, L and K are the quantities of labour and capital and f shows the functional relation between the inputs and output. The production function is based on an implicit assumption that the technology is given. This is because an improvement in technical knowledge will lead to larger output from the use of same quantity of inputs.

3.2.1 USES OF PRODUCTION FUNCTION

The production function can have various uses. It can be used to compute the least-cost factor combination for a given output or the maximum output combination for a given cost. Knowledge of production function may be helpful in deciding on the value of employing a variable factor in the production process. As long as the marginal revenue productivity of a variable factor exceeds its price, it will be profitable to increase its use. When the marginal revenue productivity of the factor becomes equal to its price the additional employment of the factor should be stopped. Since, the production function shows the returns to scale it will help in the decision making. If the returns to scale are diminishing, it is not worthwhile to increase production. The opposite will be true if the returns to scale are increasing.

3.2.2 Types of Production Function

Production function is of two different forms:

- The fixed proportion production function

- The variable proportion production function

These can be explained as follows:

1. Fixed Proportion Production Function

A fixed proportion production function is one in which the technology requires a fixed combination of inputs, say capital and labour, to produce a given level of output. There is only one way in which the factors may be combined to produce a given level of output efficiently. In this type of production, there is no possibility of substitution between the factors of production.

The fixed proportion production function is illustrated by isoquants which are 'L' shaped or 'right angle' shaped. This is shown in Fig. 3.1 below.

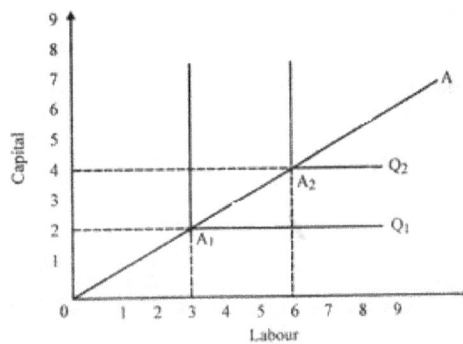

Fig. 3.1: Fixed Proportion Production Function

Let us suppose that at point A, the output is one unit. The isoquant Q_1 passing through the point A_1 shows that one unit of output is produced by using 2 units of capital and 3 units of labour. In other words, the capital-labour ratio is 2:3. In this case with 2 units of capital, any increase in labour beyond 3 units will not increase output and, therefore, labour beyond 3 units is redundant. Similarly, with 3 units of labour, any increase in capital beyond 2 units is redundant. The kink point shows the most efficient combination of factors. The capital labour ratio must be maintained for any level of output. The output can be doubled by doubling the quantity of inputs, that is, two units of output can be produced by 4

Managerial Economics   85

units of capital and 6 units of labour. Thus isoquant Q_2 passes through the point A_2. The line OA describes a production process, that is, a way of combining inputs to obtain certain output. The slope of the line shows the capital-labour ratio.

The fixed proportion production function is characterised by constant returns to scale, that is, a proportionate increase in inputs leads to a proportionate increase in outputs. This type of production function provides the basis for the input - output analysis in economics. Thus, this type of isoquant is also called input-output isoquant or "leontiff" isoquant after Leontiff who invented the input-output analysis.

2. Variable Proportions Production Function

The variable proportion production function is the most familiar production function. In this case, a given level of output can be produced by several alternative combinations of factors of production, say capital and labour. It is assumed that the factors can be combined in infinite number of ways. The common level of output obtained from alternative combinations of capital and labour is given by an isoquant Q in Fig. 3.2, given below:

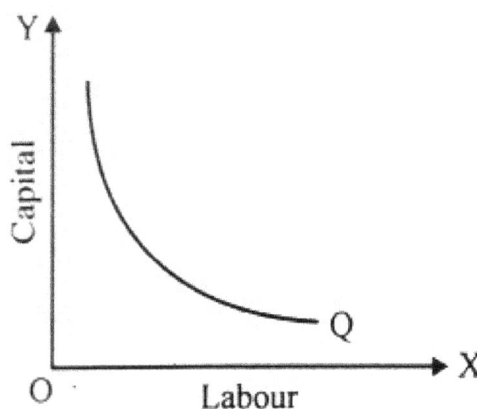

Fig. 3.2: Variable Proportions Production Function

The isoquant Q is the locus of efficient points of factor combinations to produce a given level of output. The isoquant is continuous, smooth and convex to the origin. It assumes continuous substitutability of capital and labour over a certain range, beyond which factors cannot substitute each other.

Since the variable proportions production function is the most common we discuss below in detail the isoquant representing the variable the proportions production function.

3.2.3 SHORT RUN AND LONG RUN PRODUCTION FUNCTION

The discussion of production up to now has ignored the time needed to build production facilities. There is a need to take into consideration the time factor in the discussion on the production. Thus, in this section we consider the behaviour of production in the short-run and long-run.

The short run is a phase in which the organisation can alter manufacturing by changing variable factors such as supplies and labour but cannot change fixed factors such as capital. The long run is a phase adequately long so that all factors together with capital can be altered.

The factors which can be increased in the short run are called variable factors, since they can be easily changed in a short period of time. Hence, the level of production can be increased within the limits of existing plant capacity during the short run. Thus, the short run production function proves that in the short run the output can be increased by changing the variable factors, keeping the fixed factors constant. In other words, in the short run the output is produced with a given scale of production, that is, with a given size of plant. The behaviour of production in the short-run where the output can be increased by increasing one variable factor keeping other factors fixed is called law of variable proportions.

The size of plant can be varied in the long run and, therefore, the scale of production can be varied in the long run. The long run analysis of the laws of production is referred to as laws of returns to scale.

🔔	**Study Notes**

1.   Explain Production Function.

2.   What are the uses and types of Production Function?

3.   Explain short and long run production function.

🗣	**Discussion**

Discuss which is the technically efficient method of production out of the two given in the table below, and why?

Factor inputs	Method A	Method B
Labour	5	4
Capital	4	4

3.3   Cost Function

Cost function is a derived function. It is derived from the production function, which describes the efficient method of production at any given time. The production function specifies the technical relationships between inputs and the level of output. Thus, cost will vary with the changes in the level of output, nature of production function, or factor prices. Thus, symbolically, we may write the cost function as

$C = f(X, T, P_f)$

Where, C = Total cost, X = Output, T = Technology, P_f = Prices of factors.

Total cost is evidently, an increasing function of output, $C = f(X)$, ceterius paribus. The clause 'ceteris paribus' implies that 'all other factors which determine costs are constant'. If these factors change, they will affect the cost. The technology is itself determined by the physical quantities of the factor inputs, the quality of the factor inputs, the efficiency of the entrepreneur, both in organising the physical side of the production and in making the correct economic choice of techniques. Thus, any change in these determinants will shift the production function and hence will shift the cost curve. For instance, the introduction of a better method of organising production or the application of an educational programme to the existing labour will shift the production function upwards and hence will shift down the cost curve. Similarly, the improvement of raw material, or the improvement in the use of the same raw materials will lead to a downward shift of the cost function.

Since no output is possible without an input, an increase in factor prices, ceteris paribus, will lead to an increase in the cost. The factor prices depend on the demand and supply of factors in the economy.

Of all the determinants of cost, the cost-output relationship is considered as the most important one. Thus, in economic analysis the cost function is analysed with respect to output. This is because the cost-output relationship is subject to faster and more frequent changes. The relationship between cost and output is analysed with respect to short-run and long-run.

3.3.1 SHORT RUN COST FUNCTION

In the short-run the firm cannot change or modify overhead factors such as plant, equipment and scale of its organisation. In the short-run output can be increased or decreased by changing the variable inputs like labour, raw material, etc. Thus, the short-run costs of production are segmented into fixed and variable costs. On the other hand, in the long-run all factors can be adjusted. Hence, in the long run all costs are variable and none are fixed.

1) Total Cost: Fixed and Variable

The total cost (TC) of the firm is a function of output (q). It will increase with the increase in output, that is, it varies directly with the output. In symbols, it can be written as

TC = f(q)

Since the output is produced by fixed and variable factors, the total cost can be divided into two components: total fixed cost (TFC) and total variable cost (TVC).

TC = TFC + TVC

• **Fixed Cost**

Fixed costs are those which are independent of output. They must be paid even if the firm produces no output. They will not change even if output changes. They remain fixed whether output is large or small. Fixed costs are also called 'overhead costs', 'sunk costs' or 'supplementary costs'. They comprise payments such as rent, interest, insurance, depreciation charges, maintenance costs, property taxes, administrative expense like manager's salary and so on. In the short period, the total amount of these fixed costs will not increase or decrease when the volume of the firms output rises or falls (See Table 3.3).

- **Variable Cost**

Variable costs are those which are incurred on the employment of variable factors of production. They vary with the level of output. They increase with the rise in output and decrease with the fall in output. By definition, variable costs remain zero when output is zero. They include payments for wages, raw materials, fuel, power, transport and the like. Marshall called these variable costs as "Prime Costs" of production.

The relation between total variable cost and output may not be linear, that is, variable cost may not increase by the same amount for every unit increase in output. This is shown in the table mentioned below:

Table 3.1: A Schedule of a Firm's Total Cost

Output (q) (1)	Total Fixed Cost (TFC) (2)	Total Variable Cost (TVC) (3)	Total Cost (TC) (4)
0	100	0	100
1	100	25	125
2	100	40	140
3	100	50	150
4	100	70	170
5	100	100	200
6	100	145	145
7	100	205	305
8	100	285	385

9	100	385	485
10	100	515	615

Table 3.1 shows a simplified cost schedule showing the relation between costs for each different levels output. We can observe the following relations:

- The column (2) shows that TFC remains fixed at all levels output.

- The column (3) shows that TVC varies with the output and it is zero when the output is nil. It can also be observed from the column (3) that TVC does not change in the same proportion. In the beginning, as the output increases, TVC increases at a decreasing rate, but after a point it increases at an increasing rate. This is due to the operation of the law of variable proportions.

- The column (4) shows that total costs are equal to fixed plus variable costs. TC varies with the change in output in the same proportion as the TVC.

The above costs and output relations are also shown in Fig 3.3. By plotting the cost data of Table 3.1, graphically and joining the plotted points by smooth curves, we can obtain total fixed, total variable and total cost curves.

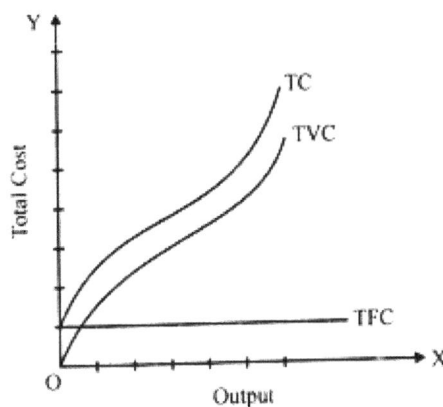

Fig. 3.3: Total Cost Curves

It can be seen from Fig 3.3 that since total fixed cost remains constant, TFC curve is parallel to the X-axis. The TVC curve begins at zero and then rises gradually in the beginning and eventually, becomes steeper as the output rises. The TC curve is obtained by adding up vertically TFC and TVC curves. The shape of the TC curve is exactly the same as that of TVC curve because the same vertical distance separates TC and TVC curves.

2) Unit Costs

There are four different kinds of unit costs, viz. average total cost (or as usually called average cost), average fixed cost, average variable cost and marginal cost.

• Average Total Cost (ATC)

One of the most important cost concepts is average total cost. When compared with price or average revenue it will allow a business to determine whether or not it is making a profit. Average total cost is total cost divided by the number of units produced i.e.

$$\text{Average Total Cost} = \frac{\text{Total Cost}}{\text{Quantity}} \quad \text{or} \quad ATC = \frac{TC}{q}$$

Since, the total cost is the sum of total fixed cost and total variable cost, the average total cost is also the sum of average fixed cost (AFC) and average variable cost (AVC). Thus, Average Total Cost (ATC) = Average Fixed Cost (AFC) + Average Variable Cost (AVC).

• Average Fixed Cost (AFC)

By dividing total fixed cost by output we get average fixed cost.

$$AFC = \frac{TFC}{q}$$

Since, the same amount of fixed cost is shared equally between the various, units of output; AFC falls continuously as output rises.

• Average Variable Cost (AVC)

Average variable cost is total variable cost divided by output. Thus,

$$AVC = \frac{TVC}{q}$$

The average variable cost will generally fall as the output rises from zero to the normal capacity level of output due to the operation of increasing returns. Beyond the normal capacity output, any increase in output will increase AVC quite sharply on account of the operation of diminishing returns.

• Marginal Cost (MC)

Marginal cost is the extra or additional cost of producing one extra unit of output. In economics the term 'marginal' whether applied to utility, cost, production, consumption or whatever means 'incremental' or 'extra'. Thus, marginal cost is the total cost of n units of output minus the total cost of n-1 units. In symbols:

$$MC_n = TC_n - TC_{n-1}$$

Since, fixed costs do not change with outputs, MC is independent of fixed cost. On the other hand, variable costs vary with output in the short-run and therefore, MC can be calculated from total variable cost. Hence, marginal cost is the addition to the total variable cost for producing an additional unit of output. In other words, marginal cost is equal to the change in TVC.

- **Computation of AC, AFC, AVC and MC**

The computation of AC, AFC, AVC and MC and their relationships are illustrated by a hypothetical example and it is shown in Table 3.2

Table 3.2: A Schedule of Short Run Costs

Quantity	Total Fixed Cost	Total Variable Cost	Total Cost	Marginal Cost	Average Total Cost	Average Fixed Cost	Average Variable Cost
Q	TFC	TVC	TC = TFC + TVC	MC	ATC = TC/q or ATC = AVC + AFC	AFC = TFC / q	AVC = TFC / q
(1)	(2)	(3)	(4)	(5)	(6)	(7)	(8)
0	100	0	100	--	--	--	--
1	100	25	125	25	125	100	25
2	100	40	140	15	70	50	20
3	100	50	150	10	50	33.3	16.7
4	100	70	170	20	42.5	25	17.5
5	100	100	200	30	40	20	20

6	100	145	145	45	40.8	16.6	24.2
7	100	205	305	60	43.6	14.3	29.3
8	100	285	385	80	48.1	12.5	35.6
9	100	385	485	100	53.9	11.1	42.8
10	100	515	615	130	61.5	10	51.5

Column (7) shows that AFC declines continuously as output increases. We can observe from column (8) that AVC falls initially, reaches a minimum and eventually rises with the increase in output. From column (6) we can see that ATC too falls initially, reaches the minimum and then rises as output increases. It can also be seen that ATC is the sum of AFC and AVC. Column (5) shows that MC too behaves in the same way as AVC and ATC.

- **Relationship between AC, AFC, AVC and MC Curves**

The relationship between AC, AFC, AVC and MC is explained graphically by drawing respective cost curves in Fig. 3.4. The behaviour of cost curves is explained below.

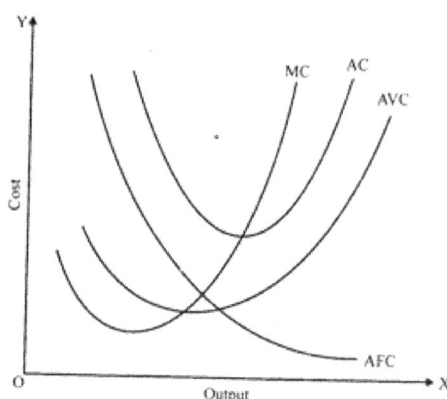

Fig. 3.4: Marginal and Average Cost Curves

Since, AFC is falling steadily as output increases, the AFC curve is also falling steadily from left to right. In mathematical terms, AFC curve approaches both axes, that is, it gets very near to but never touches either axis. Since we are dividing the constant fixed cost by different levels of output, AFC curve is a rectangular hyperbola. This implies that if we multiply AFC at any point on the AFC curve with the corresponding quantity of output, we will always get the same total fixed cost. This property of the AFC curve shows that TFC is constant throughout.

The AVC curve falls initially, reaches a minimum and then rises as output increases. It falls slowly as the firm's output rises from zero to the normal capacity level. Once normal capacity output is reached AVC curve rises sharply with the increase in output. This is owing to the fact that the use of more and more of the variable factors, say labour, will lead to overcrowding and also to problems of organisation. Further, as the existing fixed factors are used more intensively machines will breakdown more frequently. All these lead to sharp increase in AVC.

If AFC and AVC curves are added together we obtain ATC curve or, as usually called, average cost (AC) curve. In the beginning as output rises ATC curve falls because of the predominance of falling AFC curve. At higher levels of output AVC curve rises quite sharply and therefore, ATC curve rises after a point. The continuous fall in average fixed costs will be too small to offset it. Thus AC curve is 'U' shaped.

MC curve is also 'U' shaped as in Fig. 3.4. Marginal cost curve falls initially, then reaches a minimum point and finally rises. The shape of the MC curve is determined by the law of variable proportions, that is, by the behaviour of the marginal product of the variable factor. MC curve intersects AC and AVC curves at their minimum. This is due to the important relationship between marginal and average costs.

The relationship between AVC, ATC and MC can be summarised as follows:

- AVC, ATC and MC fall first, then reach a minimum and finally rise as output increases.

- The rate of change in MC is greater than that in AVC and therefore the MC is lowest at an output lower than the output at which AVC is lowest.

- The ATC falls for a longer range of output than the AVC and therefore the minimum ATC is at a larger output than the minimum AVC.

- MC = AVC, when AVC is lowest.

- MC = ATC, when ATC is minimum.

3.3.2 RELATION BETWEEN AC AND MC

The relationship between AC and MC are the following:

- If MC is below AC, then AC must be falling. This is because, if MC is below AC, then the last unit produced costs less than the AC of all the earlier units produced. If the last unit costs less than the earlier ones, then the new AC must be less than the old AC. Hence, AC must be falling.

- If MC is above AC, then the cost of the last unit produced will be higher than the AC of the earlier units. Hence, the new AC must be higher than old AC. Therefore, when MC is above AC, AC must be rising.

- If MC is equal to AC, the last unit costs exactly the same as the AC of all earlier units. Hence the new AC is equal to old AC. Thus, the AC curve is flat when AC equals MC.

The above mentioned relationship between AC and MC can be seen clearly with the help of figure 3.5

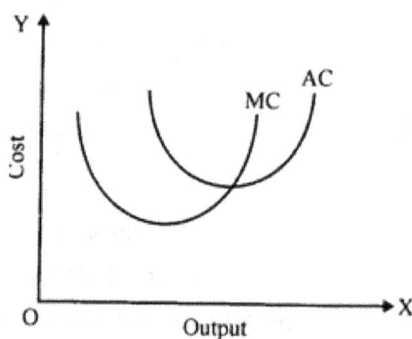

Fig. 3.5: Relation between AC and MC

To the left of the lowest point of the AC curve, MC is below AC, so the AC curve is falling. Even if MC is rising, AC will continue to fall as long as the rising MC is less than AC. To the right of the minimum point of the AC curve, MC is above AC, so the AC curve is rising. At the point where MC equals AC, the AC curve is flat. Hence the rising MC curve cuts the AC curve at its lowest point.

The relationship between AC and MC can be easily understood by an example of a cricket player's batting averages. Let us assume that a cricket player's batting average is 40. If in his next innings he scores less than 40, let us assume 30, then his average score will fall because his marginal score is less than his average score. Instead, if he scores more than 40, say 50, in his next innings, then his average score will increase because his marginal score is greater than his previous average score. On the other hand, assuming the average score is 40, if the batsman scores 40 in his next innings then his average score will remain the same and his marginal and average scores will be equal.

This relationship between average and marginal cost can easily be recalled with the aid of Fig. 3.6. It can be seen from the figure that so long as MC is below AC, average cost falls, that is, MC pulls AC downwards. When MC is above AC, the average cost rises, that is, MC pulls AC upwards. When MC equals AC, the average cost remains constant, that is, MC pulls AC horizontally. The arrows show the direction of these pulls.

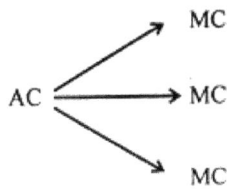

Fig. 3.6: Average and marginal cost

It is to be noted that a rising MC curve also cuts AVC curve at its lowest point. The reason for this is exactly the same as that we have given above to explain why MC cuts AC at its minimum point.

3.3.3 LONG RUN COST FUNCTION

In the long-run a firm can amend its size and organisation to volatile demand conditions. In other words, in the long-run the firm can adjust its scale of operations or size of plant to produce any required output in the most efficient way. Thus, in the long run fixed factors can be altered. Management can be restructured to run a firm of a different size. Capital can also be used differently. In short, all factors are variable in the long run and therefore the scale of operations can be altered.

Thus, in the long-run all costs are variable (i.e. the firm faces no fixed costs). The length of time of the long-run depends on the industry. In some service industries, such as dry-cleaning, the period of the long-run may be only a few months or weeks. For capital intensive industries, such as electricity-generating plant, the construction of a new plant may take many years and hence long-run may be many years. The length of time of the long-run depends upon the time required for the firm to be able to vary all inputs.

The long-run is often presented as the planning sphere as the organisation can construct the plant that cuts down the expenditure of producing any estimated level of output. Once the plant has been constructed, the organisation operates in the short-run. Therefore, the organisation plans for the long-run and operates in the short-run.

LONG RUN AVERAGE COST CURVE

In the long run, a firm can have a large number of alternative plant sizes. For a certain level of output, a plant of a particular size will be most suited.

Corresponding to each scale or size of the plant there will be an average cost curve. Hence, the long run is a series of alternative short run average cost curves, associated with different plants, out of which a choice is to be made by the firm for its actual operation. The long run average cost curve is derived from a number of short run average cost (SAC) curves. This is explained in Fig 3.7.

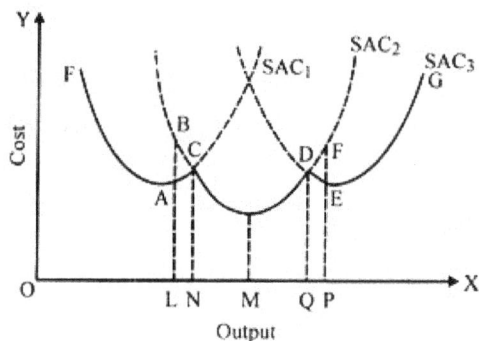

Fig 3.7: Long run Average Cost Curve

The above figure is drawn on the assumption that there are three plants and they are depicted by the short run average cost curves SAC₁, SAC₂, SAC₃. A given plant is best suited for a particular level of output. It can be seen from Fig. 3.7 that output OL can be produced at a lower cost with the plant SAC₁, than with the plant SAC₂. The cost of producing OL output on plant SAC₁, is AL and it is less than the cost of producing the same output with plant SAC₂. The difference in cost is equal to AB. If the firm wants to produce ON output it can produce it either by plant SAC₁, or plant SAC₂. But it would be advantageous for the firm to use the plant SAC₂ for ON level of output because the larger output OM can be obtained at the lowest average cost from this plant. Thus, output larger than ON but less than OQ can be produced at a lower average cost with plant SAC₂. For output larger than OQ, the firm will have to employ plant SAC₃. For instance, output OP can be produced at average cost of PE with plant SAC₃.

It is clear from the above analysis that in the long run the firm has a choice regarding the employment of a plant and it will employ that plant which yields possible minimum average cost for producing a given output. Thus long-run average cost curve depicts the lowest possible average cost for producing various levels of output. Assuming that there are only three plants as in Fig. 3.7, then LAC curve is the thick wave like portions of SAC curves, i.e., FACDEG. The dotted portions of these SAC curves are of no importance in the long-run because the firm would prefer to change the size of the plant rather than operate on them.

If we assume that the size of the plant can be varied by infinitely small gradations so that there are numerous SAC curves corresponding to infinite number of plants, the long run average cost curves will be smooth one as in Fig. 3.8. Since, we are assuming an infinite number of SAC curves, every point on the LAC curve will be a tangency point with some SAC

Managerial Economics

curve. Hence, the LAC curve is the locus of the points of the lowest average cost of producing various levels of output.

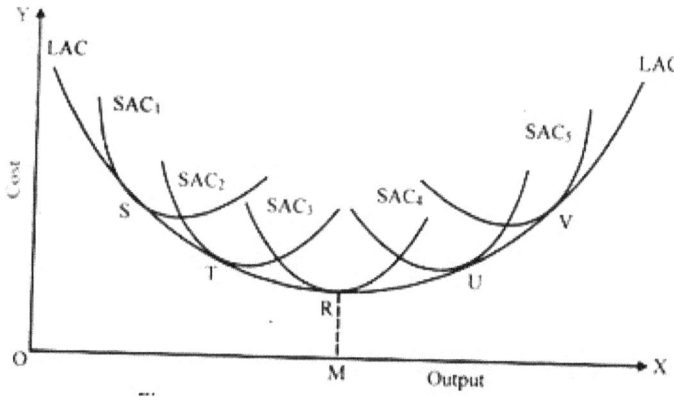

Fig 3.8: Long run Smooth Envelope Curve

It should be noted that, with one exception, the LAC curve is not tangent to the minimum points of the short run average cost curves. This exception occurs at the optimum level of output. In Fig. 3.8, this occurs at the output OM at which the lowest point of SAC_3 coincides with the minimum point on the LAC curve at point R. The plant SAC_3 which produces the optimum output OM at the minimum cost RM is the optimum plant. For outputs less than OM the lowest long run costs occur on the falling portions of SAC curves. In Fig. 3.8, LAC curve is tangent to falling portions of SAC_1 and SAC_2 at points S and T respectively, but points of S and T are not the minimum points of SAC_1 and SAC_2. On the other hand, for outputs greater than OM, the lowest long run average costs occur on the rising portions of short run average cost curves.

⚠	**Study Notes**

3.4 Production Isoquant

3.4.1 ISOQUANTS

An isoquant shows all those combinations of factors which produce the same level of output. An isoquant is also known as equal product curve or iso-product curve.

3.4.2 TYPES OF ISOQUANTS

The isoquant may have various shapes depending on the degree of substitutability of factors:

1. **Linear Isoquant:** In this case, the isoquant would be straight lines as in Fig. 3.9 This type assumes perfect substitutability of factors of production. In this case, labour and capital are perfect substitutes, that is, the rate at which labour can be substituted for capital in production is constant.

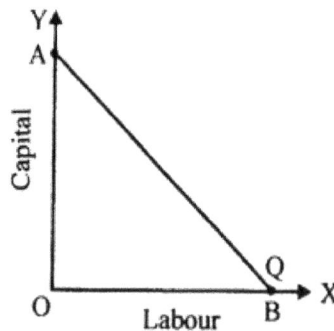

Fig. 3.9: Linear Isoquant

This isoquant evinces that a given commodity may be produced by using only capital or only labour or by an infinite combination of labour and capital. At point A on the isoquant the level of output can be produced with capital alone (i.e. without labour). Similarly, point B indicates that the same level of output can be produced with labour alone (i.e. without any capital). This is unrealistic because capital and labour are not perfectly substitutable.

2. **Right Angled Isoquant:** This assumes zero substitutability of the factors of production. There is only one method of producing any one commodity. In this case, the isoquant takes the form of a right angle as in Fig. 3.10.

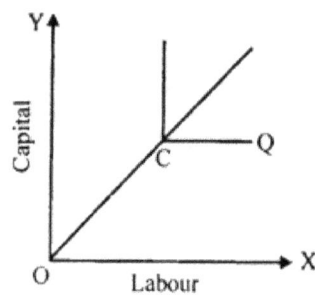

Fig. 3.10: Right Angled Isoquant

In this case, labour and capital are perfect complements, that is, labour and capital must be used in fixed proportion shown by point C. The output can be increased only by increasing both the quantity of labour and capital in the same proportion depicted at the point C.

This isoquant is called input-output isoquant or Leontief isoquant after Leontief, who invented the input-output analysis.

3. **Kinked Isoquant:** This isoquant assumes only limited substitutability of capital and labour. There are only a few processes for producing any one commodity.

This is shown in Fig. 3.11 where A_1, A_2, A_3 and A_4 show the production process and Q is the kinked isoquant. In this case, the O substitutability of factors is possible only at the kinks.

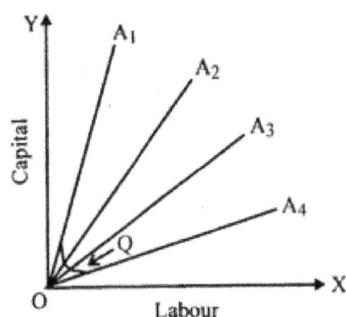

Fig. 3.11: Kinked Isoquant

This is more realistic type of isoquant because engineers, managers and production executives consider the production process as a discrete rather than continuous process.

4. **Smooth Convex Isoquant:** This type of isoquant assumes continuous substitutability of capital and labour over a certain range, beyond which the factors cannot substitute each other. This is shown in Fig 3.12.

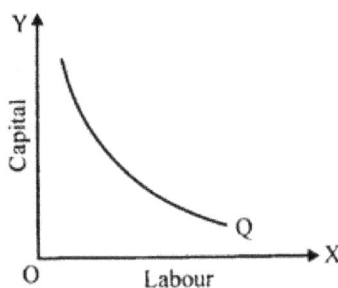

Fig. 3.12: Smooth Convex Isoquant

The traditional economic theory has adopted this isoquant for analysis since it is uncomplicated. Further, this is an approximation to the more realistic form of a kinked isoquant because as the number of process become infinite, the isoquant becomes a smooth curve. Therefore, the properties of this isoquant are explained in detail below.

DERIVATION OF SMOOTH CONVEX ISOQUANT

It is assumed that each of the different combinations of labour and capital shown in Table 3.3 produces the same level of output, that is, 20 units. The combinations are such that if one factor is increased the other factor is decreased and vice versa. All these combinations are technically efficient.

Table 3.3: Various Combinations of Labour and Capital to Produce 20 Units of Output

Factor Combination	Labour	Capital
A	1	15
B	2	11
C	3	8
D	4	6

If we plot all these combinations and join them we obtain a curve Q. This is shown in Fig 3.13.

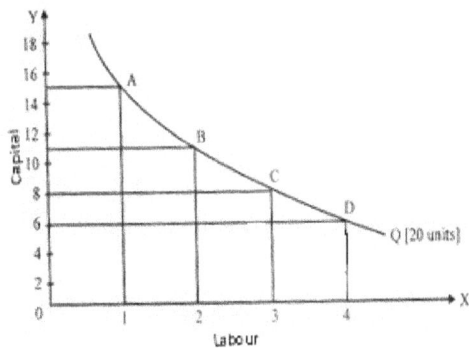

Fig. 3.13: Isoquant or Equal Product Curve

The curve Q is the isoquant or equal product curve. It shows all those combinations of labour and capital which, with a given technology, produce 20 units of output. Thus, an isoquant is the locus of all those sublimations of labour and capital, which yield the same level of output. In other words, an isoquant includes all the technically efficient methods of producing a given level of output.

Isoquant Map

We can label isoquants in physical units of output without any difficulty. Since, each isoquant represents a specified level of output it is possible to say by how much the output is greater or lesser on one isoquant than on other. This is explained by an isoquant map shown in Fig. 3.14

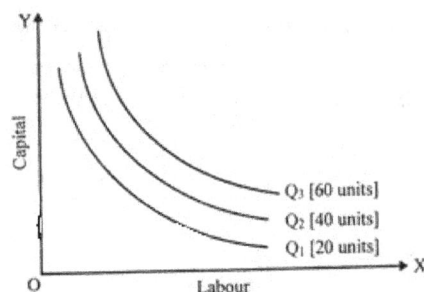

Fig. 3.14: Isoquant Map

It shows that the output is 20 units, 40 units and 60 units on isoquants Q_1, Q_2 and Q_3 respectively. Thus, on isoquant Q_2 the output is 20 units more than on isoquant Q_1; and on isoquant Q_3 the output is 40 units more than on isoquant Q_1. So, an isoquant map facilitates not only measurement of the physical quantities of output but also comparison the size of output between the various isoquants. In theory, an isoquant map contains an infinite number of isoquants. This is because the response of output to infinite changes in factors is assumed to be continuous.

3.4.3 PROPERTIES OF ISOQUANTS

The important properties of isoquants are the following:

1. **Isoquants slope downwards to the right:** It means that, in order to keep the output constant; when the amount of one factor is increased the quantity of other factor must be reduced.

   An upward sloping isoquant demonstrates that a given product can be produced with less of both the factors of production. An entrepreneur, who is maximising profits, would not use any combinations of factors shown on an upward sloping portion of an isoquant. Therefore, the points on the upward sloping portion of an isoquant cannot represent an equilibrium position. Similarly, a horizontal or vertical range of an isoquant cannot also represent a possible position of equilibrium. In this case, the same output could be obtained at a reduced cost by reducing the amount of one of the factors. Thus, isoquants slope downwards to the right as in fig 3.15.

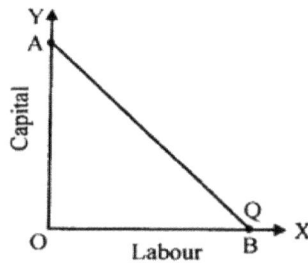

Fig. 3.15: Isoquant sloping downwards

2. **Isoquants are convex to the origin:** The slope, at any point of an isoquant, is negative. Its numerical value measures the marginal rate of technical substitution between labour and capital. It equals the ratio of the marginal product of labour to the marginal product of capital. Thus, the slope of an isoquant is

$$\frac{\Delta K}{\Delta L} = MRTS_{LK} = \frac{MP_L}{MP_K}$$

Where ΔK is the change in capital, ΔL is the change in labour, $MRTS_{LK}$ is the marginal rate of technical substitution of labour for capital, MP_L is the marginal product of labour and MP_K is the marginal product of capital.

The convexity of isoquant means that as we move down the curve less and less of capital is given up for an additional unit of labour so as to keep constant the level of output. This can be observed from the Fig. 3.16.

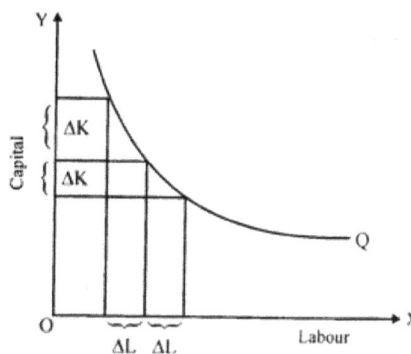

Fig. 3.16: Convex Isoquant

It can be seen from the figure above that as we increase labour at a constant rate the amount of capital given up (ΔK) for an additional unit of labour goes on falling. Thus, the convexity of the isoquant shows that the marginal rate of technical substitution of labour for capital is diminishing.

Managerial Economics   **105**

If the isoquant is concave to the origin it would mean that the marginal rate of technical substitution is increasing. This behaviour is elucidated in Fig. 3.17

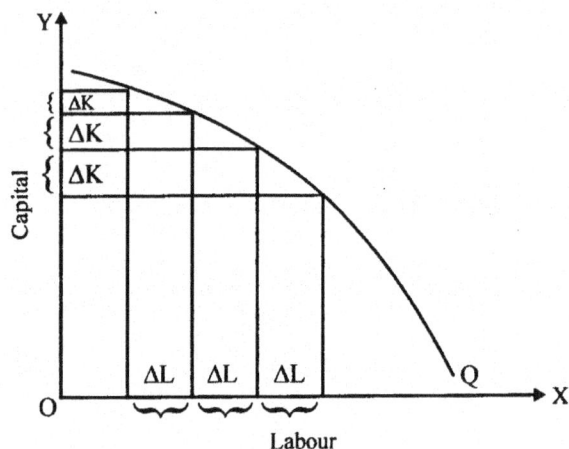

Fig 3.17: Concave Isoquant

It is apparent from the Fig. 3.17 that as the labour is increased at a constant rate the amount of capital given up (▲K) goes on increasing. Such behaviour is irrational and therefore, isoquants are not concave to the origin.

3. **Isoquants do not intersect:** By definition isoquants, like indifference curves, can never cut each other. If they cut each other it would be a logical contradiction.

4. **Isoquants cannot touch either axis:** If an isoquant touches any axis, as in Fig. 3.18 it would mean that the output can be produced with the help of one factor. It is unrealistic because output cannot be produced only by labour or capital alone.

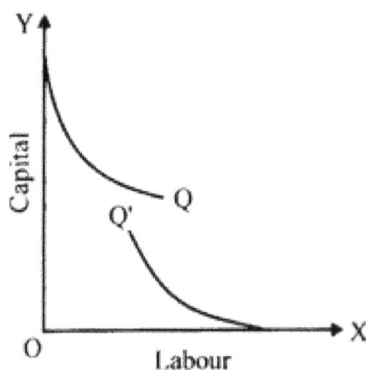

Fig 3.18: Isoquant touching axis

3.5 ISOCOST

In economics, an isocost line represents all combinations of inputs which cost the same total amount. Although, similar to the budget constraint in consumer theory, the use of the isocost line pertains to cost-minimisation in production, as opposed to utility-maximisation. For the two production inputs, labour and capital, with fixed unit costs of the inputs, the equation of the isocost line is

$$rK + wL = C$$

Where w represents the wage rate of labour, r represents the interest rate of capital, K is the amount or units of capital used, L is the amount of labour used and C is the total cost of acquiring these inputs.

The absolute value of the slope of the isocost line, with capital plotted vertically and labour plotted horizontally, equals the ratio of the prices of inputs of labour and capital. The isocost line is combined with the isoquant map to determine the optimal production. This optimality is arrived at a point where an isoquant and the isocost curves are tangent to each other. It ensures that the firm attains the highest level of possible output with a given isocost line. Consequently, the output is produced at with least cost or most efficiently. This tangency can also be interpreted as one where the slopes of the isoquant and the isocost are equal. This entails that tangency ensures that the marginal productivities of the two inputs are proportional to the ratios of the prices of the two inputs. Specifically, the point of tangency between an isoquant and an isocost line gives the lowest-cost combination of inputs that can produce the level of output associated with that.

- **Least Cost Factor Combination: Producers Equilibrium or Optimal Combination of Inputs**

   The analysis of production function has shown that alternative combinations of factors of production, which are technically efficient, can be used to produce a given level of output. Of these, the firm will have to choose that combination of factors which will cost it the least. In this way the firm can maximise its profits. The choice of any particular method from a set of technically efficient methods is an economic one and it is based on the prices of factors of production at a particular time.

   The firm can maximise its profits either by maximising the level of output for a given cost or by minimising the cost of producing a given output. In either case, the factors will have to be employed in optimal combination at which the cost of production will be minimum.

   There are two ways to determine the least cost combination of factors to produce a given output. That is,

- Finding the total cost of factor combinations

- Geometrical method

1. Finding the Total cost of Factor Combinations

   Here we try to find the total cost of each factor combination and choose the one which has the least cost. The cost of each factor combination is found by multiplying the price of each factor by its quantity and then summing it for all inputs. This is illustrated in Table 3.4.

Table 3.4: Choosing the Lowest Cost of Production Technique

Technique	Capital (units)	Labour (units)	Capital Cost Rs.	Labour Cost Rs.	Total Cost Rs.
1	2	3	4	5	6
A	6	10	500X6=3000	400X10=4000	7000
B	2	14	500X2=1000	400X14=5600	6600

It is assumed that 100 pairs of shoes are produced per week and the price of capital and the wage of labour are Rs. 500 and Rs. 400 per week respectively. In order to simplify the analysis, we assume that there are only two technically efficient methods of producing shoes and they are labelled A and B.

The table 3.4 demonstrates that the total cost of producing 100 pairs of shoes is Rs. 7000 per week using technique A and Rs. 6600 per week using technique B. The firm will choose technique B, which is an economically efficient (or lowest cost) production technique at the factor prices assumed in the above example.

If either of the factor prices alters the equilibrium proportion of the factors will also change so as to use less of those factors that display a price rise. Therefore, we will have a new optimal combination of factors. This can again be found out by calculating the cost of different factor combinations with the new factor prices and choosing the one that costs the least.

2. Geometrical method

The second and a more general way to determine the least cost combination of factors is geometrical in essence. It is done with the help of isoquant map and isocost line. In order to determine the least cost factor combination or the maximum output for a given cost, we have to superimpose the isoquant map on the isocost line. This is explained below.

a) Isoquant Map

An isoquant map shows all the possible combinations of labour and capital that can produce different levels of output. The isoquant closer to the origin denotes a lower level of output. The slope of an isoquant is

$$\frac{\Delta K}{\Delta L} = MRTS_{LK} = \frac{MP_L}{MP_K}$$

The isocost line shows various combinations of labour and capital that the firm could buy for a given amount of money at the given factor prices. This is explained in Fig. 3.19

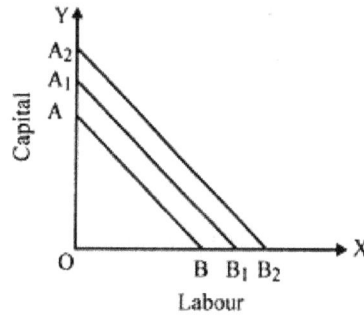

Fig. 3.19: Iso-cost Line

In the figure, the line AB is the isocost line. It depicts that the firm can hire OA amount of capital or OB amount of labour or some combinations of labour and capital along the AB line. Thus, isocost line is the locus of all those combinations of labour and capital which, given the prices of labour and capital, could be bought for a given amount of money. The slope of the isocost line is equal to the ratio of the factor prices, that is, the slope of iso-cost line.

Similar iso-cost lines can be drawn for different sums of money. If the money to be spent on the factors increase, the isocost line will shift to the right and it denotes that with the given factor prices, the firm could buy more of the factors. Thus, we can have a family of isocost lines AB, A_1B_1 and A_2B_2 as in Fig 3.19. They are all parallel to one another because the factor prices are assumed to be the same in all cases. The iso-cost lines closer to the origin show a lower total cost outlay.

b)   Slope of Isocost Line

Given the monetary resources, if the factor prices change the slope of isocost line will change. This is shown in Fig 3.20.

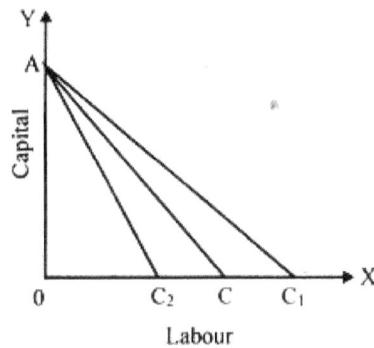

Fig. 3.20: Slope of Iso-cost Line

Let us assume that with a given amount of money and the prices of labour and capital, the iso-cost line is AC in Fig 3.20. If the price of labour falls the firm could hire more than OC amount of labour for the same amount of money. If we assume that the firm could hire only OC, amount of labour then the slope of isocost line changes to AC_1. On the other hand, if the price of labour rises, the firm could hire less than OC amount of labour. If we assume that the firm could hire only OC_2 amount of labour then the slope of iso-cost line changes to AC_2.

Thus, the iso-cost line depends upon 2 factors: (i) prices of factors of production (ii) the amount of money which the firm can spend on the factors. A change in the amount of money will shift the isocost lines as in Fig. 3.20 but the slope of iso-cost lines remains constant. A change in factor prices, for example labour will change the slope of iso-cost lines as in Fig. 3.20.

The producer can be in equilibrium either by minimising the cost of producing a given output or by maximising the level of output for a given cost. These both cases are explained below:

- **Optimal Input Combination for Minimising Cost**

In this case, the firm has to produce the given output with the minimum cost. This is explained in Fig 3.21.

The single isoquant Q denotes the desired level of output to be produced. There is a family of isocost lines AB, A_1B_1 and A_2B_2. The isocost lines are parallel because the factor prices are assumed to be constant and therefore, all the iso-cost lines have the same slope.

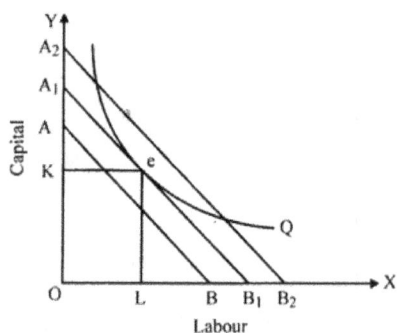

Fig. 3.21: Minimising Cost

The firm minimises its cost at the point 'e' where the isoquant Q is tangent to the isocost line AB. The optimal combination of factors is OK and OL. The optimal combination takes place at the point 'e' where the given output can be produced at the least cost. Points below 'e' are desirable but are not attainable for output Q. Points above 'e' are on higher iso-cost lines and they show higher costs. Hence, the point 'e' is the least cost point and it is the lowest cost combination of factors for producing the output Q. It is produced by OK amount of capital and OL amount of labour. At the point of tangency, that is, at point 'e', the slope of isocost line is equal to the slope of the isoquant. This is the first condition for the equilibrium. The second condition is that the isoquant should be convex to the origin at the point of equilibrium. Thus at the point 'e' the ratio of marginal product of two factors is equal to the ratio of their factor prices.

- **Optimal Input Combination For Maximisation of Output**

The equilibrium conditions of the firm are identical to the above situation that is, the iso-cost line should be tangent to the highest possible isoquant and the isoquant must be convex. However, the present problem is conceptually different. In this case the firm has to maximise its output for a given cost. This is explained in the fig. 3.22:

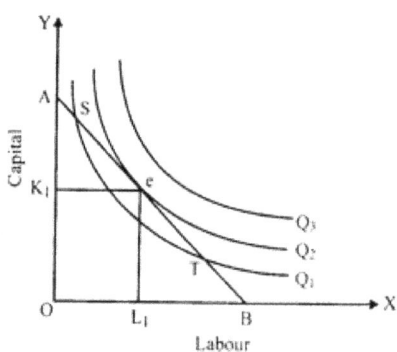

Fig. 3.22: Maximisation of Output

The firm's cost constraint is given by the iso-cost line AB. The maximum level of output that the firm can produce is Q_2 because the point 'e' lies on the isoquant Q_2. The point 'e' is the equilibrium point because at this point the iso-cost line AB is tangent to the isoquant Q_2. Other points on the isocost line that is S and T, lie on a lower isoquant Q_1. Points to the right of 'e' indicate higher levels of output which are desirable, but are not attainable due to the cost constraint. Hence, Q_2 is the maximum output possible for the given cost. The optimal combination of factors is OK_1 and OL_1.

The above analysis shows that the optimal combination of inputs needed for a firm to minimise the cost of producing a given level of output or to maximise the output for a given cost outlay is given at the tangency point of an isoquant and is cost line.

The above analysis is based on constant factor prices. If the factor prices change, the firm will choose another factor combination that will minimise the cost of production for the given output or maximise the level of output for a given cost.

🔔	**Study Notes**

👁	**Assessment**
1.	What is Iso-cost?
2.	Explain Least Cost Factor Combination.

🗣	**Discussion**
Discuss Geometrical Method in detail.	

3.6 Economies of Scale

3.6.1 CONCEPT OF ECONOMIES OF SCALE

Economies of scale allude to the cost advantages that a business obtains due to expansion. 'Economies of scale' is a long run concept and refers to reductions in unit cost as the size of a facility and the usage levels of inputs increases. Diseconomies of scale are the opposite. The common sources of economies of scale are labour (division of labour) purchasing (bulk buying of materials through long-term contracts), managerial (increasing the specialisation of managers), financial (obtaining low interest loans when borrowing from banks and having access to a greater range of financial instruments), marketing (spreading the cost of advertising over a greater range of output in media markets) and technological (taking advantage of returns to scale in the production function). Each of these factors reduces the long run average costs (LRAC) of production by shifting the short-run average total cost (SRATC) curve down and to the right. Economies of scale are also derived partially from learning by doing.

Before explaining economies and diseconomies of scale, let us have a look at laws of returns to scale, in brief.

3.6.2 LAWS OF RETURNS TO SCALE

Laws of returns to scale refer to the long-run analysis of the laws of production. In the long run, output can be increased by varying all factors. Thus, in this section we study the changes in output as a result of changes in all factors. In other words, we study the behaviour of output in response to changes in the scale. When all factors are increased in the same proportion an increase in scale occurs.

Scale refers to quantity of all factors which are employed in optimal combinations for specified outputs. The term 'returns to scale' refers to the degree by which output changes as a result of a given change in the quantity of all inputs used in production. We have three types of returns to scale: constant, increasing and decreasing. If output increases by the same proportion as the increase in inputs we have constant returns to scale. If output increases more than proportionally with the increase in inputs, we have increasing returns to scale. If output increases less than proportionally with the increase in inputs we have decreasing returns to scale. Thus, returns to scale may be constant, increasing or decreasing depending upon whether output increases in the same, greater or lower rate in response to a proportionate increase in all inputs. Returns to scale can be expressed as a movement along the scale line or expansion path which we have seen in the previous section. The three types of returns to scale are explained below.

1.   Constant Returns to Scale

If output increases in the same proportion as the increase in inputs, returns to scale are said to be constant. Thus, doubling of all factor inputs causes doubling of the level of output; trippling of inputs causes trippling of output and so on. The case of constant returns to scale is sometimes called linear homogenous production function. This is illustrated with the help of isoquants in Fig. 3.23 where the line OE is the scale line. The scale line indicates the increase in scale. It can be observed from Fig. 3.23 that the distance between successive isoquants is equal, that is, Oa = ab = bc. It means that if both labour and capital are increased in a given proportion the output expands in the same proportion.

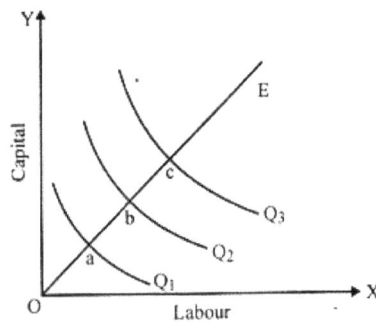

Fig 3.23: Constant returns to Scale: Oa=ab=bc

2.   Increasing returns to scale

When the output increases at a greater proportion than the increase in inputs, returns to scale are said to be increasing. It is explained in Fig. 3.24. When the returns to scale are increasing, the distance between successive isoquants becomes less and less, that is, Oa >ab >bc. It means that equal increases in output are obtained by smaller and smaller increments in inputs. In other words, by doubling inputs the output is more than doubled.

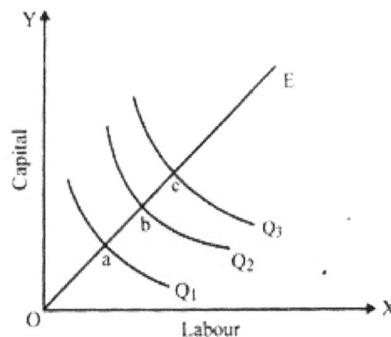

Fig. 3.24: Increasing returns to scale: Oa>ab>bc

Increasing returns to scale arise on account of indivisibilities of some factors. As output is increased the indivisible factors are better utilised and therefore, increasing returns to scale arise. In other words, the returns to scale are increasing due to economies of scale.

3.   Decreasing returns to scale

When the output increases in a smaller proportion than the increase in all inputs returns to scale are said to be decreasing. It is explained in Fig. 3.24.

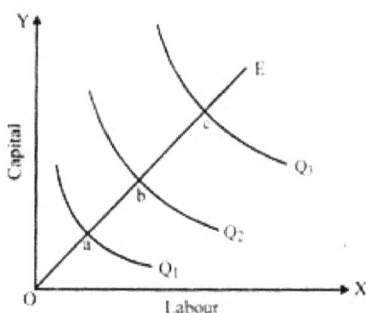

Fig. 3.25: Decreasing returns to scale: Oa<ab<bc

It can be seen from Fig. 3.24 that the distance between successive isoquants are increasing, that is, Oa < ab < bc. It signifies that equal increments in output are obtained by larger and larger increases in inputs. In other words, if the inputs are doubled, output will increase by less than twice its original level. The decreasing returns to scale are caused by diseconomies of large scale production.

The returns to scale can be measured in terms of the coefficient of output elasticity (QE).

$$\textbf{Co-efficient of Output Elasticity (QE)} = \frac{\textbf{Percentage Change in Output}}{\textbf{Percentage Change in all Inputs}}$$

If QE = 1, we have constant returns to scale, if QE > 1, we have increasing returns to scale and if QE < 1, we have decreasing returns to scale.

According to economic theory, as the size of a firm increases, the firm will face successively increasing returns, followed by constant returns and then decreasing returns to scale. This is due to indivisibility of some factors. An input is said to be indivisible when it is available in a 'lumpy' form, which cannot be divided into smaller units. Therefore, as output is increased indivisible factors are better utilised and therefore, increasing returns are obtained. If the inputs are perfectly divisible we cannot have varying returns to scale, that is, returns to scale will be constant always. Thus, the existence of varying returns to scale is owing to the fact that inputs are not perfectly divisible. According to Chamberlin, the indivisibility thesis does not afford a complete explanation for the existence of increasing returns to scale. Even if all inputs are perfectly divisible the efficiency of the firm still depends upon its size. According to him, the existence of larger quantity of inputs allows for improved division of labour which, in turn, results in increasing returns to scale. Thus, as the size of the firm expands it is possible to employ superior and more efficient inputs which cause increasing returns to scale. On the other hand, decreasing returns to scale arise on account of the increasing difficulties involved in coordinating the multiplicity of complex activities of the firm. As the size of the firm increases the multiple activities of the firm become more and more complex.

The increasing and decreasing returns to scale describe the behaviour of long run average cost. The long-run average costs decrease as output rises due to increasing returns to scale (or economies of scale). The economies of scale refer to the situation in which output grows proportionately faster than inputs. For example, output more than doubles with a doubling of inputs. If the input prices remain constant, this leads to lower cost per unit. On the other hand, the long run average costs increase as output rises due to decreasing returns to scale, (or diseconomies of scale). In this case, output grows at a proportionately lower rate than the inputs. With the prices of inputs remaining constant, this leads to higher costs per unit. This leads to rising LAC (Long-run Average Cost) curve. The LAC becomes lowest at the output at which the forces for increasing returns to scale are just balanced by the forces for decreasing returns to scale.

3.6.3 ECONOMIES AND DISECONOMIES OF SCALE

Economies and diseconomies of scale are of two types- internal and external. Internal economies and diseconomies are those which a firm reaps as a result of its own expansion. On the other hand, external economies and diseconomies are those which a firm accrues as a result of the growth of industry as a whole. They are external because they accrue to the firms from outside.

The internal economies and diseconomies of scale affect the shape of the long run average cost curve. Internal economies of scale cause the long run average cost to fall, while internal diseconomies of scale causes the long run average cost to rise as output increases. On the other hand, external economies and diseconomies of scale affect the position of both the short run and long run average cost curves. External economies shift down the cost curve, while external diseconomies shift up the cost curve.

1. Internal Economies of Scale

Internal economies of scale are the advantages of large scale production. They are enjoyed by the firm when it increases its scale of production. They accrue to the firm from their own actions. They affect the shape of the long-run average cost curve. They are responsible for increasing returns to scale. According to many economists, internal economies arise due to indivisibility of some factors. As the output increases the large indivisible factors can be used more efficiently and, therefore, the firm experiences increasing returns to scale. The internal economies of scale are classified into two, as shown in the chart below:

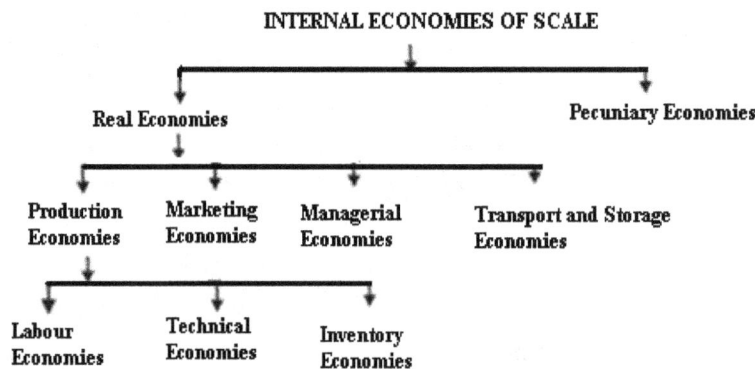

INTERNAL ECONOMIES OF SCALE

- Real Economies
  - Production Economies
    - Labour Economies
    - Technical Economies
    - Inventory Economies
  - Marketing Economies
  - Managerial Economies
  - Transport and Storage Economies
- Pecuniary Economies

Fig. 3.26: Chart representing Internal Economics of Scale

A) REAL ECONOMIES OF SCALE

Real economies are delineated as those which are associated with a reduction in the physical quantity of inputs such as raw materials, varying types of labour and various types of capital. They are mostly associated with indivisibilities or lumpiness of units of factors of production. The important kinds of real economies are:

1. Production economies

2. Marketing economies

3. Managerial economies

4. Transport and storage economies

1. **Production Economies**: Production economies arise from the use of factors of production in the form of (i) labour economies (ii) technical economies and (iii) inventory economies

- **Labour Economies:** As the size of output increases the firm enjoys labour economies due to (a) specialisation, (b) time-saving, (c) automation of the production process and (d) 'cumulative volume' economies. As the size of production increases the firm merits from the advantages of division of labour and specialisation of labour which enhance the productivity of the various types of labour. The advantages of division of labour is emphasised by Adam Smith in his book, *The Wealth of Nations* published in 1776. Division of labour also condenses the time lost in changing from one type of work to another. Division of labour promotes invention of tools and machines which, in turn, leads to mechanisation of the production process. This assists the labour in working faster and therefore, increases the labour productivity. Further, large scale production helps the technical personnel to acquire considerable experience from the 'cumulative effect'. This 'cumulative volume' experience leads to higher productivity. Hence, as the size of output increases the unit cost falls.

- **Technical Economies:** The important technical economies result from the use of specialised capital equipment, which comes into effect only when the output is produced on a large scale. Technical economies also arise from the indivisibilities, which are the characteristics of the modern techniques of production. In other words, as the scale of production increases the firm reaps the advantages of mechanisation of using mass production methods. This will reduce the unit cost of production.

- **Inventory Economies:** The role of inventories is to aid the firm in meeting random changes in the input and the output sides of the operations of the firm. The purpose of inventories is to smooth out the supply of inputs and the supply of outputs. Inventories on spare parts, raw materials and finished products increase with the scale of production, but they do not increase proportionately with the increase in the size of output. Therefore, as the size of output amplifies the firm can hold smaller percentage of inventories to meet random changes.

2. **Marketing Economies:** They are allied with the selling of the product of the firm. They arise from advertising economies. Since, advertising expenses increase less than proportionately with the increase in output, the advertising costs per unit of output falls as the output increases. Similarly, other sales promotion expenditures like samples, salesmen force etc. also increase less than proportionately with the output. Further, a large firm can have special arrangements with exclusive dealers to maintain a good service department for the product of the firm. Hence, the average selling costs fall with the increase in the size of the firm.

3. **Managerial Economies:** Large scale production makes possible the division of managerial functions. Thus, there exists a production manager, a sales manager, a finance manager, a personnel manager and so on in a large firm. However, all or most of the managerial decisions are taken by a single manager in a small firm. This division of managerial functions increases their efficiency. The decentralisation of managerial decision making also increases the efficiency of management. Large firms are also in a position to introduce mechanisation of managerial functions through the use of telex machines, computers and so on. Hence, as output increases the managerial costs per unit of output continue to decline.

4. **Transport and Storage Economies:** As the output increases, the unit cost of transportation of raw materials, intermediate products and finished products fall. This is because a large firm may be able to reduce transport costs by having their own transportation means or by using larger vehicles. Similarly, as the size of the firm increases the storage costs will also fall.

B) PECUNIARY ECONOMIES

Pecuniary economies (i.e. monetary economies) are those economies accrued by the firm from paying lower prices for the factors used in production and distribution of the product due to bulk buying by the firm. They add to the firm on account of discounts it can obtain due to its large scale production. They reduce the money costs of the factors for a particular firm.

The pecuniary economies are realised by a firm in the following ways:

- The firm will be able to get raw materials at lower prices due to bulk buying.

- A large firm can get funds at lower cost, that is, at a lower rate of interest due to its reputation in the money market.

- The large firm may be given lower advertising rates if they advertise at large.

- Transport rates may be also low if the amount of commodities transported is large.

2. Internal Diseconomies of Scale

Internal economies of scale exist only up to a certain size of the plant. This size of plant is known as the optimum plant size because with this size of plant all possible economies of scale will be fully exploited. If the size of the plant increases beyond this optimum size there arise diseconomies of scale (i.e. decreasing returns to scale) especially from managerial diseconomies. It is argued that technical diseconomies can be avoided by duplicating the optimum technical size of the plant.

The most important cause for diseconomies of scale is the diminishing returns to management. As the output grows beyond certain level the top management becomes overburdened, it becomes less efficient as coordinator and ultimate decision maker. Thus, increase in the size of the plant beyond a certain large size makes the managerial structure more complicated and reduces the overall efficiency of the management.

Another cause for diseconomies of scale may be the exhaustible natural resources. E.g., increasing the fishing fleet may not cause an increase in catching of the fish.

3. External Economies

The external economies arise outside the firm as a result of improvement in the industrial environment in which the firm operates. They are external to the firm, but internal to the industry to which the firms belong. They may be realised from the actions of other firms in the same industry or in another industry. Their effect is to cause a change in the prices of factors employed by the firm. They cause a shift in the short-run and long-run cost curves of the firm.

The important external economies are the following:

- **Cheapening of Materials and Equipments:** Expansion of an industry increases the demand for various kinds of materials and capital equipments. This will lead to large scale production of materials and equipments. Large scale production will reduce their cost of production and therefore, their prices. Hence, the firms using them will get them at lower prices.

- **Growth of Technical Know-how:** Expansion of an industry may lead to the discovery of new technical know-how. As a result of this the firms may be able to use improved and better machinery which will increase the productivity of the firms and therefore, reduce the cost of production.

- **Development of Skilled Labour:** As the industry grows the training facilities for labour will increase. This helps the development of skilled labour, which will increase the productivity of workers in the firms.

- **Growth of Subsidiary and Ancillary Industries:** Expansion of an industry may facilitate the growth of subsidiary and ancillary industries to produce tools, equipments, machines etc. and to provide them to the main industry at the lower prices. Likewise, firms may also come up to transform the waste of the industry into some useful products. This tends to reduce the cost of production.

- **Development of Transportation and Marketing Facilitates:** The expansion of an industry may expedite the development of transportation and marketing facilities which will reduce the cost of transportation.

- **Development of Information Services:** External economies also arise from the interchange of technical information between firms. With the expansion of an industry the firms may give the information about the technical knowledge through the publication of trade and technical journals. The firms may also set up jointly research institutes to develop new improved techniques.

4. External Diseconomies

The expansion of an industry is likely to generate external diseconomies which raise the cost of production. An increase in the size of industry may raise the prices of some factors like raw materials and capital goods which are in short supply. Expansion of an industry may also elevate the wages of skilled labour, which are in short supply. It may also create transport bottlenecks. As the size of an industry expands lakes, rivers and seas may be polluted by firms. This will create external diseconomies to some other firms or industries, for example, the fishing industry. Pollution of this sort will also create health hazards to the people in the adjoining areas. Expansion of an industry may also pollute the air from the smoke of factories or fumes of vehicles. This too will have similar diseconomies.

Thus, several external diseconomies may be generated by the expansion of the size of an industry (or industries) and they will raise the costs of the individual firms.

⚠	**Study Notes**

| (eye icon) | **Assessment** |

Write notes on the following:

1. Concept of Economies of Scale

2. Internal Economies of Scale

3. Internal Diseconomies of Scale

4. External Economies of Scale

5. External Diseconomies of Scale

| (face icon) | **Discussion** |

Discuss Laws of Returns to scale in detail.

3.7 Summary

Production Function: A production function specifies the output of a firm, an industry or an entire economy for all possible combinations of inputs. This function is an assumed technological relationship, based on the current state of engineering knowledge and technical feasibility of substituting inputs.

TYPES OF PRODUCTION FUNCTION

Production function is of two different forms:

- The fixed proportion production function

- The variable proportion production function

These can be explained as follows:

1. Fixed Proportion Production Function

A fixed proportion production function is one in which the technology requires a fixed combination of inputs, say capital and labour, to produce a given level of output. There is only one way in which the factors may be combined to produce a given level of output efficiently. In this type of production, there is no possibility of substitution between the factors of production.

The fixed proportion production function is characterised by constant returns to scale, that is, a proportionate increase in inputs leads to a proportionate increase in outputs. This type of production function provides the basis for the input - output analysis in economics. Thus, this type of isoquant is also called input-output isoquant or "leontiff" isoquant after Leontiff who invented the input-output analysis.

2. Variable Proportions Production Function

The variable proportion production function is the most familiar production function. In this case, a given level of output can be produced by several alternative combinations of factors of production, say capital and labour. It is assumed that the factors can be combined in infinite number of ways.

Cost Function: The term cost function is a financial term used by economists and mangers within businesses to understand how costs behave. The cost function shows how a cost changes as the levels of an activity relating to that cost changes.

Cost function is a derived function. It is derived from the production function, which describes the efficient method of production at any one time. In other words, the production function specifies the technical relationships between inputs and the level of output. Thus, cost will vary with the changes in the level of output, nature of production function, or factor prices. Thus, symbolically, we may write the cost function as

$C = f(X, T, P_f)$

Where, C = Total cost, X = Output, T = Technology, P_f = Prices of factors.

Isoquants: An isoquant is the locus of points showing how a given output can be produced with different combinations of inputs. An isoquant shows the extent to which the firm in question has the ability to substitute between the two different inputs in order to produce the same level of output.

Types of Isoquants

1. Linear isoquant

2. Right angled isoquant

3. Kinked isoquant

4. Smooth convex isoquant

Isocost: An isocost line shows all possible combinations of inputs which cost the same total amount. Although similar to the budget constraint in consumer theory, the use of the isocost line pertains to cost-minimisation in production, as opposed to utility-maximisation.

Economics of Scale: Economies of scale, refers to the cost advantages that a business obtains due to expansion. There are factors that cause a producer's average cost per unit to fall as the scale of output is increased. "Economies of scale" is a long run concept and refers to reductions in unit cost as the size of a facility and the usage levels of other inputs increase.

3.8   Self Assessment Test

Broad Questions

1. What is production function? Discuss the fixed proportions and variable proportions production functions.

2. Explain the concept of isoquant. What are the properties of isoquants?

3. The firm can maximise its profits by choosing the least cost combination of factors. Discuss.

4. The firm can maximise its profits by employing the factors in optimal combinations at which the cost of production will be minimum. Explain.

5. Discuss diagrammatically the laws of returns to scale.

Short Notes

    a. Production function

    b. Isoquant

    c. Isocost line

    d. Expansion path

    e. Economies of scope

    f. Internal economies of scale

3.9 Further Reading

1. Business Economics, Adhikary, M,., Excel Books, New Delhi, 2000

2. Economics Theory and Operations Analysis, Baumol, W J., 3rd ed., Prentice Hall Inc, 1996

3. Managerial Economics, Chopra, O P., Tata McGraw Hill, New Delhi, 1985

4. Managerial Economics, Keat, Paul G and Philips K Y Young, Prentice Hall, New Jersey, 1996

5. A Modern Micro Economics, Koutsoyiannis, Macmillan, 1991

6. Economics Organisation and Management, Milgrom, P and Roberts J, Prentice Hall Inc,Englewood Clitts, New Jersey, 1992

7. Managerial Economics, Maheshwari, Yogesh, Sultanchand and Sons, 2009

8. Managerial Economics, Varshney, R L., Sultanchand and Sons, 2007

Assignment

Quote examples, how can production and cost functions be used in daily life?

_____

_____

_____

_____

_____

_____

_____

_____

_____

_____

_____

_____

_____

_____

_____

_____

_____

_____

_____

_____

_____

_____

_____

_____

Unit 4　Theory of Firm

	Learning Outcome

After going through this unit, you will be able to:

- Discuss various theories of firm

- Describe transaction cost theory

- Outline Managerial and Behavioural Theories

- Describe Williamson's approach

- Distinguish Profit and Sales Maximisation

- Define Team Production

	Time Required to Complete the unit

1. 1st Reading: It will need 3 Hrs for reading a unit

2. 2nd Reading with understanding: It will need 4 Hrs for reading and understanding a unit

3. Self Assessment: It will need 3 Hrs for reading and understanding a unit

4. Assignment: It will need 2 Hrs for completing an assignment

5. Revision and Further Reading: It is a continuous process

	Content Map

4.1　Introduction

4.2　Theory of Firm

4.3　Various Theories of Firm

　　4.3.1　Transaction Cost Theory

	4.3.2	Managerial and Behavioural Theories
	4.3.3	Profit Maximisation
	4.3.4	Sales Maximisation
	4.3.5	Team Production
	4.3.6	Williamson's Approach
	4.3.7	Simon Satisfying Behaviour Model
	4.3.8	Other Models
4.4	**Summary**	
4.5	**Self Assessment Test**	
4.6	**Further Reading**	

4.1 Introduction

Microeconomics, especially the theory of the firm, assumed importance and attracted considerable attention in the early twentieth century. This shift ensued after the growing realisation that perfect competition assumption of the classical economists was not a ground reality. This realisation resulted in a spate of efforts to analyse and understand the behaviour of individual firms. In perfect competition, all firms are assumed to be price takers and therefore studies into the behaviour of individual firms were not called for. Since, the reality was far different, the urgency to study the behaviour of firms of all sizes was obvious. Naturally theory of the firm, rather how firms, big and small, behave under different circumstances began to attract wide attention, especially in the aftermath of World War I.

The need for a revised theory of the firm was emphasised by empirical studies undertaken by Berle and Means, which made it clear that ownership of a typical American corporation is spread over a wide number of shareholders, leaving control in the hands of managers who own very little equity themselves. Hall and Hitch found that executives made decisions by rule of thumb rather than in accordance to marginal analyses. Firms exist as an alternative system to the market mechanism when it is more efficient to produce in a non-price environment. For example, in a labour market, it might be very difficult or costly for firms or organisation to engage in production when they have to hire and fire their workers depending on demand/supply conditions. It might also be costly for employees to shift companies everyday looking for better alternatives. Thus, firms engage in a long-term contract with their employees to minimise the cost.

Klein (1983) asserts that "Economists now recognise that such a sharp distinction [between intra- and inter-firm transactions] does not exist and that it is useful to consider also transactions occurring within the firm as representing market (contractual) relationships". The costs involved in such transactions that are within a firm or even between the firms are transaction costs.

According to Putterman, this is an exaggeration—most economists accept a distinction between the two forms, but also that the two merge into each other; the extent of a firm is not simply defined by its capital stock. Richardson for example, notes that a rigid distinction fails because of the existence of intermediate forms between firm and market such as inter-firm co-operation.

Ultimately, whether the firm constitutes a domain of bureaucratic direction that is shielded from market forces or simply "a legal fiction", "a nexus for a set of contracting relationships among individuals" (Jensen and Meckling) is "a function of the completeness of markets and the ability of market forces to penetrate intra-firm relationships".

4.2 Theory of Firm

Theory of the firm is related to comprehending how firms come into being, what are their objectives, how they behave and improve their performance and how they establish their credentials and standing in society or an economy and so on. The theory of the firm aims at answering the following questions:

- Existence – why do firms emerge and exist, why are not all transactions in the economy mediated over the market?

- Which of their transactions are performed internally and which are negotiated in the market?

- Organisation – why are firms structured in such a specific way? What is the interplay of formal and informal relationships?

- Heterogeneity of firm actions/performances – what drives different actions and performances of firms?

⚠	**Study Notes**

👁	**Assessment**
Write a note on the history of Theory of Firms.	

🗣	**Discussion**
Discuss the aims of theory of Firm.	

4.3 Various theories of Firm

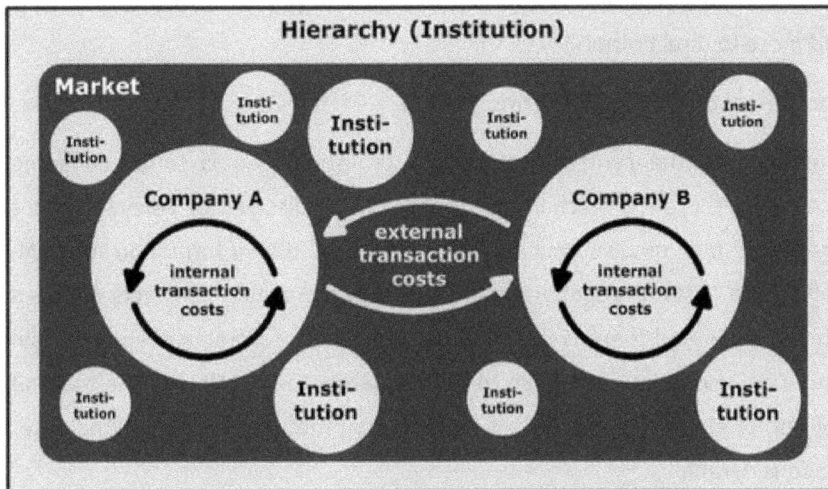

Fig. 4.1: Transaction Cost Theory

The above model reveals institutions and market as a possible form of organisation to coordinate economic transactions. When the external transaction costs are higher than the internal transaction costs, the company will grow. If the external transaction costs are lower than the internal transaction costs the company will be downsized by outsourcing. For example, Ronald Coase set out his transaction cost theory of the firm in 1937, making it one of the first (neo-classical) attempts to define the firm theoretically in relation to the market. Coase sets out to define a firm in a manner which is both realistic and compatible with the idea of substitution at the margin, so instruments of conventional economic analysis apply. He notes that a firm's interactions with the market may not be under its control (for instance because of sales taxes), but its internal allocation of resources is: "Within a firm, market transactions are eliminated and in place of the complicated market structure with exchange transactions is substituted the entrepreneur who directs production". He asks why alternative methods of production (such as the price mechanism and economic planning), could not either achieve all production, so that either firms use internal prices for all their production, or one big firm runs the entire economy.

Coase begins from the standpoint that markets could in theory carry out all production and that what needs to be explained is the existence of the firm, with its "distinguishing mark ... [of] the supersession of the price mechanism". Coase identifies some reasons why firms might arise and dismisses each as unimportant:

- If some people prefer to work under direction and are prepared to pay for the privilege (but this is unlikely)

- If some people prefer to direct others and are prepared to pay for this (but generally people are paid more to direct others)

- If purchasers prefer goods produced by firms

Coase contends that the central reason to establish a firm is to evade some transaction costs of using the price mechanism. These include discovering relevant prices (which can be reduced but not eliminated by purchasing this information through specialists), as well as the costs of negotiating and writing enforceable contracts for each transaction (which can be large if there is uncertainty). Moreover, contracts in an uncertain world will necessarily be incomplete and have to be frequently re-negotiated. The costs of haggling about division of surplus, particularly if there is asymmetric information and asset specificity, may be considerable.

If a firm operated internally under the market system, many contracts would be required (for instance, even for procuring a pen or delivering a presentation). In contrast, a real firm has very few (though much more complex) contracts, such as defining a manager's power of direction over employees, in exchange for which the employee is paid. These kinds of contracts are drawn up in situations of uncertainty, in particular for relationships which last long periods. Such a situation runs counter to neo-classical economic theory. The neo-classical market is instantaneous, forbidding the development of extended agent-principal (employee-manager) relationships, of planning and of trust. Coase concludes that "a firm is likely therefore to emerge in those cases where a very short-term contract would be unsatisfactory". and that "it seems improbable that a firm would emerge without the existence of uncertainty".

He notes that government measures relating to the market (sales taxes, rationing, price controls) tend to increase the size of firms, since firms internally would not be subject to such transaction costs. Thus, Coase defines the firm as "the system of relationships which comes into existence when the direction of resources is dependent on the entrepreneur". We can therefore think of a firm as getting larger or smaller based on whether the entrepreneur organises more or fewer transactions.

However, what determines the size of the firm; why does the entrepreneur organise the transactions he does, why no more or less? Since, the reason for the firm's being is to have lower costs than the market, the upper limit on the firm's size is shaped by costs mounting to the point where internalising an additional transaction equals the cost of making that transaction in the market. (At the lower limit, the firm's costs exceed the market's costs and it does not come into existence.) In practice, diminishing returns to management, augments cost of organising a large firm, particularly in large firms with many different plants and differing internal transactions (such as a conglomerate) or if the relevant prices change recurrently.

Coase concludes that the size of the firm is reliant on the costs of using the price mechanism and on the costs of organisation of other entrepreneurs. These two factors collectively determine how many products a firm produces and how much of each product they produce.

4.3.2 MANAGERIAL AND BEHAVIOURAL THEORIES

It was only in the 1960s that the neo-classical theory of the firm was disputed by alternatives such as managerial and behavioural theories. Managerial theories of the firm, as developed by William Baumol (1959 and 1962), Robin Marris (1964) and Oliver E. Williamson (1966), suggest that managers would seek to maximise their own utility and consider the implications of this for firm behaviour in contrast to the profit-maximising case. Baumol suggested that managers' interests are best served by maximising sales after achieving a minimum level of profit which satisfies shareholders. More recently this has developed into 'principal-agent' analysis (e.g. Spence and Zeckhauser and Ross (1973) on problems of contracting with asymmetric information) which models a widely applicable case where a principal (a shareholder or firm for example) cannot infer how an agent (a manager or supplier, say) is behaving. This may arise either because the agent has greater expertise or knowledge than the principal or because the principal cannot directly observe the agent's actions; it is asymmetric information which transforms into a problem of moral hazard. This means that to an extent, managers can pursue their own interests. Traditional managerial models typically assume that managers, instead of maximising profit, maximise a simple objective utility function (this may include salary, perks, security, power, prestige) subject to an arbitrarily given profit constraint (profit satisfying).

4.3.3 PROFIT MAXIMISATION

The profit maximisation theory states that firms (companies or corporations) will establish factories where they see the potential to achieve the highest total profit. The company will select a location based upon comparative advantage (where the product can be produced the cheapest). The theory draws from the characteristics of the location site: land price, labour costs, transportation costs and access, environmental restrictions, worker unions, population etc. The company will then elect the best location for the factory to maximise profits. This is anathema to the idea of social responsibility because firms will place their factory to achieve profit maximisation. They are nonchalant to environment conservation, fair wage policies and exploit the country. The only objective is to earn more profits. In economics, profit maximisation is the process by which a firm determines the price and output level that returns the greatest profit. There are several approaches to this problem. The total revenue–total cost method relies on the fact that profit equals revenue minus cost. Equating marginal revenue and marginal cost is a better and convenient method for arriving at profit maximising output. It allows firms to check whether they are really maximising profits at a given level of output by comparing additional costs and revenues generated by the production of an additional unit of output. If this cost of producing an additional unit is less than the addition it makes to total revenue, the firm must expand as it would increase total profit. This expansion must continue till MR and MC are equal. Profits are maximised when this equality is achieved provided the marginal cost at this level of output envelops the average cost of the firm. In case MC turns out to be higher than the marginal revenue at the point of investigation, the firm must contract by reducing its output to a level where MC equals MR. This method is particularly useful to very large organisations, with multiple divisions and where computation of total revenue and total cost may be a difficult and complex task.

a)   Total cost-total revenue method

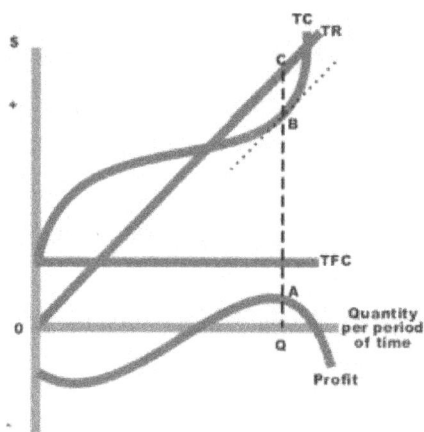

Fig. 4.2: Profit Maximisation - The Totals Approach

To obtain the profit maximising output quantity, we start by recognising that profit is equal to total revenue (TR) minus total cost (TC). Given a table of costs and revenues at each quantity, we can either compute equations or plot the data directly on a graph. Finding the profit-maximising output is as simple as finding the output at which profit reaches its maximum. That is represented by output Q in the diagram.

There are two graphical ways of determining that Q is optimal. Firstly, we see that the profit curve is at its maximum at this point (A). Secondly, we see that at the point (B) that the tangent on the total cost curve (TC) is parallel to the total revenue curve (TR), the surplus of revenue net of costs (B, C) is the greatest. Because total revenue minus total costs is equal to profit, the line segment C, B is equal in length to the line segment A, Q.

Computing the price, at which the product should be sold, requires knowledge of the firm's demand curve. Optimum price to sell the product is the price at which quantity demanded equals profit-maximising output.

b)   Marginal cost-marginal revenue method

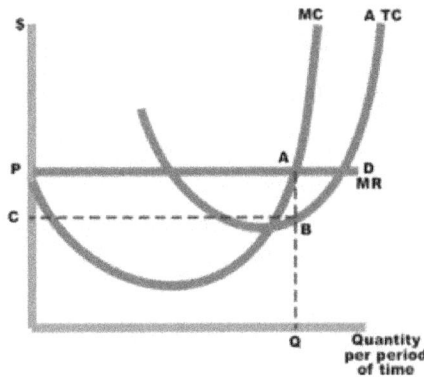

Fig. 4.3: Profit Maximisation - The Marginal Approach

An alternative argument says that for each unit sold, marginal profit (Mπ) equals marginal revenue (MR) minus marginal cost (MC). Then, if marginal revenue is greater than marginal cost, marginal profit is positive, and if marginal revenue is less than marginal cost, marginal profit is negative. When marginal revenue equals marginal cost, marginal profit is zero. Since total profit increases when marginal profit is positive and total profit decreases when marginal profit is negative, it must reach a maximum where marginal profit is zero - or where marginal cost equals marginal revenue. If there are two points where this occurs, maximum profit is achieved where the producer was collected positive profit up until the intersection of MR and MC (where zero profit is collected), but would not continue to after, as opposed to vice versa, which represents a profit minimum. In calculus terms, the correct intersection of MC and MR will occur when:

$$\frac{dMR}{dQ} < \frac{dMC}{dQ}$$

The intersection of MR and MC is shown in the next diagram as point A. If the industry is perfectly competitive (as is assumed in the diagram), the firm faces a demand curve (D) that is identical to its Marginal revenue curve (MR), and this is a horizontal line at a price determined by industry supply and demand. Average total costs are represented by curve ATC. Total economic profit are represented by area P,A,B,C. The optimum quantity (Q) is the same as the optimum quantity (Q) in the first diagram.

If the firm is operating in a non-competitive market, minor changes would have to be made to the diagrams. For example, the Marginal Revenue would have a negative gradient, due to the overall market demand curve. In a non-competitive environment, more complicated profit maximization solutions involve the use of game theory.

c)   Maximising revenue method

In some cases, a firm's demand and cost conditions are such that marginal profits are greater than zero for all levels of production. In this case, the $M\pi = 0$ rule has to be modified and the firm should maximise revenue. In other words, the profit maximising quantity and price can be determined by setting marginal revenue equal to zero. Marginal revenue equals zero when the marginal revenue curve has reached its maximum value. An example would be a scheduled airline flight. The marginal costs of flying the route are negligible. The airline would maximise profits by filling all the seats. The airline would determine the p-max conditions by maximising revenues.

Numerical Example

A promoter decides to rent an arena for concert. The arena seats 20,000. The rental fee is 10,000. (This is a fixed cost.) The arena owner gets concessions and parking and pays all other expenses related to the concert. The promoter has properly estimated the demand for concert seats to be Q = 40,000 - 2000P, where Q is the quantity of seats and P is the price per seat. What is the profit maximising ticket price?

As the promoter's marginal costs are zero, the promoter maximises profits by charging a ticket price that will maximise revenue. Total revenue equals price, P, times quantity. Total revenue is expressed as a function of quantity, so we need to work with the inverse demand curve:

$P(Q) = 20 - Q / 2000$

This gives total revenue as a function of quantity, TR (Q) = P (Q) x Q, or

$TR(Q) = 20Q - Q^2 / 2000$

Total revenue reaches its maximum value when marginal revenue is zero. Marginal revenue is the first derivative of the total revenue function: MR (Q)=TR'(Q). So

$MR (Q) = 20 - Q / 1000$

Setting MR (Q) = 0 we get

$0 = 20 - Q / 1000$

$Q = 20,000$

Recall that price is a function of quantity sold (the inverse demand curve. So to sell this quantity, the ticket price must be

$P (20000) = 20 - 20,000 / 2,000 = 10$

It may seem more natural to view the decision as price setting rather than quantity setting. Generally, this is not a more natural mathematical formulation of profit maximisation because costs are usually a function of quantity (not of price). In this particular example, however, the promoter's marginal costs are zero. This means the promoter maximises profits simply by charging a ticket price that will maximise revenue. In this particular case, we characterise total revenue as a function of price:

$TR2 (P) = (40,000 - 2000P)P = 40,000P - 2000 (P) 2$

Total revenue reaches its maximum value when marginal revenue is zero. Marginal revenue is the first derivative of the total revenue function. So

$MR2 (P) = 40,000 - 4000P$

Setting MR2 = 0 we get,

$0 = 40,000 - 4000P$

$P = 10$

Profit = TR2 (P) -TC

Profit = [40,000P - 2000(P) 2] - 10,000

Profit = [40,000(10) - 2000(10)2] - 10,000

Profit = 400,000 - 200,000 - 10,000

Profit = 190,000

What, if the promoter had charged 12 per ticket?

Q = 40,000 - 2000P.

Q = 40,000 - 2000(12)

Q = 40,000 - 24,000 = 16,000 (tickets sold)

Profits at 12:

Q = 16,000(12) = 192,000 - 10,000 = 182,000

d)   Changes in fixed costs and profit maximisation

A firm maximises profit by operating where marginal revenue equals marginal costs. A change in fixed costs has no effect on the profit maximising output or price. The firm merely treats short term fixed costs as sunk costs and continues to operate as before. This can be confirmed graphically. Using the diagram, illustrating the total cost total revenue method, the firm maximises profits at the point where the slope of the total cost line and total revenue line are equal. A change in total cost would cause the total cost curve to shift up by the amount of the change. There would be no effect on the total revenue curve or the shape of the total cost curve. Consequently, the profit maximising point would remain the same. This point can also be illustrated using the diagram for the marginal revenue marginal cost method. A change in fixed cost would have no effect on the position or shape of these curves.

- What if the arena owner in the example above triples the fee for the next concert but all other factors are the same. What price should the promoter now charge for tickets in light of the fee increase?

    The same price of Rs. 10

    The fee is a fixed cost, which the promoter should consider a sunk cost and simply ignore it in calculating his profit maximising price. The only effect is that the promoter's profit will be reduced by Rs. 20, 000.

e)   Markup pricing

In addition to using the above methods to determine a firm's optimal level of output, a firm can also set price to maximise profit. The optimal markup rules are:

$(P - MC)/P = 1/ -E_p$

Or

$P = (E_p/(1 + E_p)) MC$

Where MC equals marginal costs and E_p equals price elasticity of demand. E_p is a negative number. Therefore, $-E_p$ is a positive number.

The rule here is that the size of the markup is inversely related to the price elasticity of demand for a good.

f) MPL, MRPL and profit maximisation

The general rule is that firm maximises profit by producing that quantity of output where marginal revenue equals marginal costs. The profit maximisation issue can also be approached from the input side. That is, what is the profit maximising usage of the variable input? To maximise profits, the firm should increase usage "up to the point where the input's marginal revenue product equals its marginal costs". So mathematically the profit maximising rule is $MRP_L = MC_L$. The marginal revenue product is the change in total revenue per unit change in the variable input- assuming input as labour. That is, $MRP_L = \Delta TR/\Delta L$. MRP_L is the product of marginal revenue and the marginal product of labour or $MRP_L = MR \times MP_L$.

- Derivation:

$MR = \Delta TR/\Delta Q$

$MP_L = \Delta Q/\Delta L$

$MRP_L = MR \times MP_L = (\Delta TR/\Delta Q) \times (\Delta Q/\Delta L) = \Delta TR/\Delta L$

4.3.4 SALES MAXIMISATION

The notion that business firms (especially those operating in the real world) are primarily goaded by the aspiration to achieve the greatest possible level of sales, rather than profit maximisation needs due consideration. On an everyday basis, most real world firms probably do try to maximise sales rather than profit. For firms operating in relatively competitive markets, facing relatively fixed prices and relatively constant average cost, then increasing sales is bound to increase profits as well.

Sales maximisation theory is an alternative theory to profit maximisation. W.J. Baumol (Economic Theory and Operations Analysis, 1965) is generally recognised as having first suggested that firms often seek to maximise the money value of their sales, i.e. their sales revenue, subject to a constraint that their profits do not fall short of some minimum level which is just on the borderline of acceptability. In other words, so long as profits are at a satisfactory level, management will devote its energy and efforts to the expansion of sales. Such a goal may be explained perhaps by the businessman's desire to maintain his competitive position, which is partly reliant on the sheer size of his enterprise. This goal may also rise out of management's vested interest since the management's salaries may be related more closely to the size of the firm's operation than to its profits, or it may simply be a matter of prestige. It is also Baumol's view that short-run revenue maximisation may be consistent with long-run profit maximisation and revenue maximisation can be regarded as a long-run goal in many oligopolistic firms. Baumol also reasons that high sales attract customers to popular products.

4.3.5 TEAM PRODUCTION

Armen Alchian and Harold Demsetz's analysis of team production is an amplification and clarification of earlier work by Coase. According to them, the firm develops because extra output is provided by team production. However, its success is conditioned according to the propensity to manage the team. This takes in to account metering problems (it is costly to measure the marginal outputs of the cooperating inputs for reward purposes) and attendant shirking (the moral hazard problem), which can be overcome by estimating marginal productivity by observing specifying input behaviour. Therefore such monitoring is essential. However, this kind of monitoring can only be encouraged effectively if the monitor is the recipient of the activity's residual income (otherwise the monitor would have to be monitored, *ad infinitum*). Thus, for Alchian and Demsetz, the firm, is an entity which brings together a team which is more productive working together than at arm's length through the market, because of informational problems associated with monitoring of effort. In effect, therefore, this is a 'principal-agent' theory. Since it is asymmetric information within the firm, which Alchian and Demsetz emphasise, it must be overcome. In Barzel's (1982) theory of the firm, drawing on Jensen and Meckling (1976), the firm emerges as a means of centralising monitoring and thereby avoiding costly redundancy in that function.

The weakness in Alchian and Demsetz's argument, according to Williamson, is that their concept of team production has quite a narrow range of application, as it assumes outputs cannot be related to individual inputs. In practice, this may have limited applicability (small work group activities, the largest perhaps a symphony orchestra), since most outputs within a firm (such as manufacturing and secretarial work) are separable, so that individual inputs can be rewarded on the basis of outputs. Hence, team production cannot offer the explanation of why firms (in particular, large multi-plant and multi-product firms) exist.

4.3.6 WILLIAMSON'S APPROACH

For Oliver E. Williamson, the existence of firms derives from 'asset specificity' in production, where assets are specific to each other such that their value is much less in a second-best use. This leads to problems if the assets are owned by different firms (such as purchaser and supplier). The reason behind it is that it will lead to protracted bargaining concerning the gains from trade because both agents are likely to become locked in a position where they are no longer competing with a (possibly large) number of agents in the entire market and the incentives are no longer there to represent their positions honestly:

Managerial Economics

large-number bargaining is transformed into small-number bargaining.

If the transaction is a recurring or lengthy one, a continual power struggle takes place concerning the gains from trade, further increasing transaction costs. Thus, re-negotiation may be necessary. Moreover, there are liable to be situations where a purchaser may require a particular, firm-specific investment of a supplier, which would be profitable for both. However, after the investment has been made it becomes a sunk cost and the purchaser can endeavour to re-negotiate the contract such that the supplier may make a loss on the investment (this is the hold-up problem, which occurs when either party asymmetrically incurs substantial costs or benefits before being paid for or paying for them). In this kind of a situation, the most efficient approach to overcome continual conflict of interest between two agents (or coalitions of agents) may be the removal of one of them from the equation by takeover or merger. Asset specificity can also apply to some extent to both physical and human capital so that the hold-up problem can also occur with labour (e.g. labour can threaten a strike because of the lack of good alternative human capital but equally the firm can threaten to fire).

Probably, the best constraint on such opportunism is reputation (rather than the law, because of the difficulty of negotiating, writing and enforcement of contracts). If a reputation for opportunism significantly damages an agent's dealings in the future, this alters the incentives to be opportunistic.

Williamson opines that the limit on the size of the firm is partly an outcome of costs of delegation (as a firm's size increases its hierarchical bureaucracy does too) and partly the result of the large firm's increasing inability to replicate high-powered incentives of residual income of an owner-entrepreneur. To a certain extent this can be attributed to the nature of large firms to ensure that its existence is more secure and less dependent on the actions of any one individual (increasing the incentives to shirk) and because intervention rights from the centre characteristic of a firm tend to be accompanied by some form of income insurance to compensate for the lesser responsibility, thereby diluting incentives. Milgrom and Roberts (1990) show that increased cost of management is a result of employee's tendency to provide false information beneficial to themselves, which increases the cost of filtering information. This grows worse with firm size and more layers in the hierarchy. Empirical analyses of transaction costs have rarely attempted to measure and operationalise transaction costs. Research that attempts to measure transaction costs is the most critical limit to efforts to potential falsification and validation of transaction cost economics.

4.3.7 SIMON SATISFYING BEHAVIOUR MODEL

The behavioural approach, as developed in particular by Richard Cyert and James G. March of the Carnegie School, places emphasis on explaining how decisions are taken within the firm and goes well beyond neo-classical economics. This approach utilises the work of Herbert Simon on behaviour in situations of uncertainty conducted in the 1950s. He argues that "people possess limited cognitive ability and so can exercise only 'bounded rationality' when making decisions in complex, uncertain situations". Thus, individuals and groups tend to 'satisfy'—that is, to attempt to attain realistic goals, rather than maximise a utility or profit function. Cyert and March argued that the firm cannot be regarded as a monolith, because different individuals and groups within it have their own aspirations and conflicting interests and that firm behaviour is the weighted outcome of these conflicts. Organisational mechanisms (such as 'satisfying' and sequential decision-taking) exist to maintain conflict at levels that are not unacceptably detrimental. Compared to ideal state of productive efficiency, there is organisational slack (Leibenstein's X-inefficiency).

For Cyert and March, the firm is best viewed as a coalition of individuals or groups of individuals. Individuals or groups of individuals are seen as being likely to have goals, whereas organisations do not. There is the likelihood that there may be competing goal conflict between individuals or groups that make up the coalition. A simple resolution of this potential conflict can be achieved as follows: The assumption that there is a supreme authority that is willing and able to force conformity in the behaviour of these individuals or groups to some higher level goal or the assumption of a happy coincidence of consensus is rejected from the outset. Rather Cyert and March argue that organisational goals are formed through a bargaining process involving the members of the coalition. The form, which this bargaining takes, is normally over the distribution of what are referred to as 'side payments'. Side payments are inducements in the form of policy commitments or simply payments. The distinction between these two forms of 'side payments' might not be important. This is because commitments to pay money can be reduced to policy commitments.

The pattern of policy commitments that result from the bargaining process can be seen to be a specification of the goals of the organisation. However, it is likely that because of the way in which agreement is reached, organisational objectives that emerge are imperfectly rationalised and expressed either in the form of 'aspiration levels' or in non-operational form. These organisational goals change in two ways as the bargaining process, which is continuous, proceeds: aspiration levels with respect to existing goals i.e. the levels of achievement regarded as acceptable by coalition members, will be modified in the light of the levels actually achieved and new goals will be introduced as the attention focus of coalition members alters. The organisation copes with irrationalised conflicting goals partly because some of the objectives are expressed in non-operational form, since at any one time some of the objectives will assume a non-active form but mainly because objectives are considered sequentially and not simultaneously. Sequential, rather than simultaneous consideration is one of the central characteristics of the theory. Closely allied to the hypothesised ability of the organisation to survive in the face of conflicting goals is the concept of 'organisational slack' i.e. the notion that due to ignorance and market imperfections, the payment made to coalition members will normally be in excess of that needed to keep them within the coalition. The existence of organisational slack enables the organisation to survive adverse changes in the external environment without disintegrating.

Decisions taken within the organisation are explicitly made dependent on the information available to and the expectations formed by the decision takers within the organisation. Emphasis is placed upon the fact that the expectations, formed on the basis of any given information and indeed the type of information gathered, will not be independent of the subjective situation and interests of the individuals or groups involved. The theory argues that change is typically only considered when a problem arises, although it is recognised that if a solution comes to hand, a search for an appropriate problem may be induced. Once a problem has arisen, usually in relation to the non achievement of one of the organisational goals or sub-goals, 'search activity' is triggered off to discover possible solutions; that is, information is sought. Here, at this point, the concept of sequential as opposed to simultaneous consideration becomes relevant. The alternatives thrown up by search activity are considered in turn as they arise and the first alternative that enables the aspiration level with respect to the goal in question to be achieved is accepted. Hence, the procedure of decision making has been described as 'satisfying' rather than maximising; it is designed to satisfy multiple, changing, acceptable-level goals, not to maximise a consistently specified objective function. This is not to say that the firm's behaviour is 'irrational'. Given the problems of information gathering and processing and the desire to reduce uncertainty, some sort of satisfying procedure may be the best possible in practice. For this reason, the approach outlined here has been nominated as 'qualified' or 'bounded' rationality.

The result of this analysis is that the firm is seen as an adaptive organisation. Changes in the environment raise problems and the organisation reacts to these problems according to certain established routines, known as 'standard operating procedures', which have been evolved in the course of a long-run adaptive process. The theory has been developed deliberately for the analysis of short-run behaviour and consequently little attention has been paid to the exploration of the long-run adaptive process.

THE SIGNIFICANCE OF THE BEHAVIOURAL APPROACH

The significance of the behavioural approach is difficult to assess. It provides useful insights into some aspects of business behaviour. Cyert and March have claimed considerable short-run predictive success with their theory and have suggested that this is due to the realism of their assumptions about the internal workings of the firms in question. However several problems are yet to be resolved. In order to predict any specific firm's behaviour, detailed knowledge of the goals and standard operating procedures of that specific firm is required. Since operating procedures in particular are by their nature highly particularised, there is little scope for generalisation. Changes in goals and standard operating procedures occur in response to fairly immediate problems, within an essentially short-run framework. Of course, the changes are made in accordance with higher level rules, but these somehow just emerge from a long-run adaptive process that is not explored and they are presumably still very firm specific. Although not explored, it is clear that the long-run adaptive process is not to be regarded as tending towards long-run 'rationality', since in an uncertain and unstable environment; it has been argued short run adaptation is the key. There may, nevertheless, be interest in the relationship between the short-run and the long run and it has yet to be demonstrated that the behavioural approach can be adapted in this direction. Associated with the short-run orientation of the behavioural approach is its concept of the firm as essentially passive. The stress on the process of short-run response to environmental stimuli, with longer-run considerations of survival conditions and strategic planning explicitly excluded is overwhelming. Yet, as argued earlier in this chapter, the characteristics of the large dominant firm suggest the need for a concept of the firm as an active entity, consciously seeking to influence its environment in ways that are favourable to the achievement of its objectives. By focusing the way in which stimuli from an exogenous environment call forth responses from an isolated individual firm, attention is firmly directed away from the properties of the system as a whole. The environment exists somehow 'out there' and its properties are placed beyond the scope of the inquiry.

It is, of course, possible to recognise the force of the observation that large firms are complex organisations and yet to avoid recourse to behaviour. If a firm's organisational characteristics have no implications for its behaviour or more probably have implications that can be taken into account without adopting a behaviourist approach, a holistic concept of the firm can be retained. Thus, although organisational characteristics such as the relationship between shareholders and managers may need to be analysed in order to determine what the firm's objective is, once this has been done, the firm can be viewed as a unit acting consistently in pursuit of a clearly specified objective. Similarly, internal administrative processes can be regarded as a separate area of study, in the same way that technical processes of production or marketing are regarded as separate areas of study and can be abstracted from the theory of the firm. Of course, the study of internal administration may lead to conclusions with relevance for a theory of the firm, such as that there exists an absolute size or a rate of growth above which the administrative efficiency of the firm declines. Once established, these conclusions can be regarded as part of the initial set of assumptions required for the construction of any theory.

The main contribution of the behavioural approach for the development of an understanding of business behaviour is to highlight the role played by uncertainty (not risk), the view that the behaviour of the firm can best be understood as viewing it as a continuing process and the rejection of micro equilibrium.

4.3.8 OTHER MODELS

Efficiency wage models like that of Shapiro and Stiglitz (1984) suggest wage rents as an addition to monitoring, since this gives employees an incentive not to shirk their responsibilities, given a certain probability of detection and the consequence of being fired. Williamson, Wachter and Harris (1975) suggest promotion incentives within the firm as an alternative to morale-damaging monitoring, where promotion is based on objectively measurable performance. (The difference between these two approaches may be that the former is applicable to a blue-collar environment, the latter to a white-collar one). Leibenstein (1966) sees a firm's norms or conventions, dependent on its history of management initiatives, labour relations and other factors, as determining the firm's 'culture' of effort, thus affecting the firm's productivity and hence size.

George Akerlof (1982) develops a gift exchange model of reciprocity, in which employers offer wages unrelated to variations in output and above the market level and workers develop concern for each other's welfare, such that all put in effort above the minimum required but the more able workers are not rewarded for their extra productivity; again, size here depends not on rationality or efficiency but on social factors. Therefore, the limit to the firm's size is given where costs rise to the point where the market can undertake some transactions more efficiently than the firm.

👁	**Assessment**

Write short notes on the following:

1. Transaction Cost Theory

2. Williamson's Approach

3. Simon Satisfying Behaviour Model

🗣	**Discussion**

Discuss the difference between PROFIT MAXIMISATION AND SALES MAXIMISATION THEORIES.

4.4 Summary

Theory of Firm: The theory of the firm consists of a number of economic theories, which describe the nature of the firm, its objectives, its existence, its behaviour and its relationship with the market.

Transaction Cost Theory: Ronald Coase set out his transaction cost theory of the firm in 1937, making it one of the first (neo-classical) attempts to define the firm theoretically in relation to the market.

Coase concludes by saying that the size of the firm is dependent on the cost of using the price mechanism and on the cost of organisation of other entrepreneurs. These two factors together determine how many products a firm produces and how much of each.

Managerial and Behavioural Theories: Managerial theories of the firm, as developed by William Baumol (1959 and 1962), Robin Marris (1964) and Oliver E. Williamson (1966), suggest that managers would seek to maximise their own utility and consider the implications of this for firm behaviour in contrast to the profit-maximising case. (Baumol suggested that managers' interests are best served by maximising sales after achieving a minimum level of profit, which satisfies shareholders.)

Profit Maximisation Theory: The profit maximisation theory states that companies or corporations will locate firms/ factories where they can achieve the highest total profit. The company will select a location based upon comparative advantage (where the product can be produced the cheapest). In economics, profit maximisation is the process by which a firm determines the price and output level that returns the greatest profit.

Sales Maximisation Theory: W.J. Baumol (Economic Theory and Operations Analysis, 1965) is generally recognised as having first suggested that firms often seek to maximise the money value of their sales i.e. their sales revenue, subject to a constraint that their profits do not fall short of some minimum level which is just on the borderline of acceptability.

Team Production: Armen Alchian and Harold Demsetz's analysis of team production is an extension and clarification of earlier work by Coase. Thus, according to them, the firm emerges because extra output is provided by team production but that the success of this depends on being able to manage the team so that metering problems (it is costly to measure the marginal outputs of the co-operating inputs for reward purposes) and attendant shirking (the moral hazard problem) can be overcome, by estimating marginal productivity by observing or specifying input behaviour.

Williamson's Approach: For Oliver E. Williamson, the existence of firms derives from 'asset specificity' in production, where assets are specific to each other such that their value is much less in a second-best use.

Simon's Satisfying Behavioural Model: Herbert Simon's work in the 1950s concerning behaviour in situations of uncertainty, which argued that "people possess limited cognitive ability and so can exercise only 'bounded rationality' when making decisions in complex, uncertain situations".

4.5 Self Assessment Test

Broad Questions

1. Explain Simon's Satisfying Behavioural Model. What is the significance of behavioural approach?

2. What are the various theories of Firm?

Short Notes

    a. Profit maximisation

    b. Transaction Cost Theory

    c. Team production

    d. Williamson's approach

    e. Sales maximisation

4.6 Further Reading

1. A Modern Micro Economics, Koutsoyiannis, Macmillan, 1991

2. Business Economics, Adhikary, M,., Excel Books, New Delhi, 2000

3. Economics Organisation and Management, Milgrom, P and Roberts J, Prentice Hall Inc, Englewood Clitts, New Jersey, 1992

4. Economics Theory and Operations Analysis, Baumol, W J., 3rd ed., Prentice Hall Inc, 1996

5. Managerial Economics, Chopra, O P., Tata McGraw Hill, New Delhi, 1985

6. Managerial Economics, Keat, Paul G and Philips K Y Young, Prentice Hall, New Jersey, 1996

7. Managerial Economics, Maheshwari, Yogesh, Sultanchand and Sons, 2009

8. Managerial Economics, Varshney, R L., Sultanchand and Sons, 2007

Assignment

According to you, which approach should be preferred, "profit maximisation or sales maximisation"? You can also suggest any other theory, which you feel should be followed.

_____

_____

_____

_____

_____

_____

_____

_____

_____

_____

_____

_____

_____

_____

_____

_____

_____

_____

_____

_____

Unit 5   Market Structure

<table>
<tr><td>◎</td><td>Learning Outcome</td></tr>
</table>

After going through this unit, you will be able to:

- Outline Classification of Market

- Discuss Meaning and characteristics of Perfect Competition.

- Interpret basics of Monopoly

- Identify Monopolistic Competition

- Outline basics of Oligopoly

- Contrast price determination in various market situations

<table>
<tr><td>🕐</td><td>Time Required to Complete the unit</td></tr>
</table>

1.   1st Reading: It will need 3 Hrs for reading a unit

2.   2nd Reading with understanding: It will need 4 Hrs for reading and understanding a unit

3.   Self Assessment: It will need 3 Hrs for reading and understanding a unit

4.   Assignment: It will need 2 Hrs for completing an assignment

5.   Revision and Further Reading: It is a continuous process

<table>
<tr><td>📄</td><td>Content Map</td></tr>
</table>

5.1   Introduction

5.2   Types of Market Structures formed by the Nature of Competition

5.3   Perfect Competition

    5.3.1   Definition of Perfect Competition

    5.3.2   Characteristics of Perfect Competition

5.3.3   Price under Perfect Competition

5.4   Monopoly

5.4.1   Definition of Monopoly

5.4.2   Characteristics of Monopoly

5.4.3   Types of Monopoly

5.4.4   Sources of Monopoly

5.4.5   Price under Monopoly

5.5   Monopolistic Competition

5.5.1   Features of Monopolistic Competition

5.5.2   Assumptions of Monopolistic Competition

5.5.3   Price determination under Monopolistic Competition

5.5.4   Defects or Wastes of Monopolistic Competition

5.6   Oligopoly

5.6.1   Definition of Oligopoly

5.6.2   Characteristics of Oligopoly

5.6.3   Price-Output Determination under Oligopoly

5.7   Summary

5.8   Self Assessment Test

5.9   Further Reading

5.1 Introduction

Market economy pricing is conditioned by market structure. There are distinct forms of market structures. Perfect competition is accorded great importance as a market structure. As a theoretical mode, classical and neoclassical economists assume conditions of perfect competition.

The market is an assemblage of conditions in which buyers and sellers come in contact for the purpose of exchange. Market situations vary in their structure. Different market structures channel the behaviour of buyers and sellers (firms). Further, different prices and trade volumes are fashioned by different market structures. Again, all kinds of markets are not equally efficient in the exploitation of resources and consumers' welfare also varies accordingly. Hence, the aspects of pricing process should be analysed in relation to different types of market.

5.2 Types of Market Structures formed by the Nature of Competition

Traditionally, the nature of competition is assayed to be the fundamental criterion for distinguishing different types of market structures.

The degrees of competition may vary among the sellers as well as the buyers in different market situations.

- The nature of competition among the sellers is viewed on the basis of two major aspects: The number of firms in the market

- The characteristics of products, such as whether the products are homogeneous or differentiated

Individual seller's control over the market supply and his hand on price determination basically depends upon these two factors.

Based on selling or supply, the following types of market structures are commonly distinguished:

- Perfect competition

- Monopoly

- Oligopoly

- Monopolistic competition

Perfect competition and monopoly are two extremes of market situations. Other forms of market such as oligopoly and monopolistic competition fall in between these two extremes. Oligopoly and monopolistic competition are the market situations characterised by imperfect competition.

⚠	**Study Notes**

👁	**Assessment**

1. Define Market.

2. What is Market Structure?

3. What are the types of Market structures on the basis of competition.

🗣	**Discussion**

Discuss Types of Market Structures Formed by the criterion other than nature of competition.

5.3 Perfect Competition

5.3.1 DEFINITION OF PERFECT COMPETITION

1. Prof. Marshall   "The more nearly perfect a market is, the stronger is the tendency for the same price to be paid for the same thing at the same time in all parts of the market".

2. Prof. Benham   "A market is said to be perfect when all the potential sellers and buyers are promptly aware of the price at which transactions take place and all of the offers made by other sellers and buyers and when any buyer can purchase from any seller and vice-versa".

Thus, perfect competition is a market situation where a colossal amount of buyers as well as sellers possessing complete knowledge of the market come together to afford the similar products. In perfect competition, an equilibrium price exists in the market and firms are free to take part in and to exit the market.

5.3.2 CHARACTERISTICS OF PERFECT COMPETITION

Following are the characteristics of perfect competition market:

- **Large Number of Buyers and Sellers:** As there are a large number of buyers and sellers, no individual buyer or seller can influence the price of product, which is determined by collective effect of all the buyers and sellers.

- **Homogenous Product:** As the product of all the firms is homogenous or identical, all the firms sell their product at the market price. No firm can charge any price more than the price prevailing in the market.

- **Free Entry and Exit of Firms:** All the firms are free to join or leave industry. There is no restriction on their entry and exit. Hence, if the industry is accruing profits, new firms will enter into the market. Contrarily, if the industry is suffering loss, many firms will leave the market.

- **Perfect Knowledge of Market Conditions**: Since all the buyers and sellers hold perfect knowledge of all the market conditions, there is free movement of buyers and sellers. Advertisement and selling methods do not have an effect on consumer behaviour.

- **Perfect Mobility of the Factors of Production**: As all the factors of production are perfectly mobile, factors of production are free to shift to any organisation where they are not being paid a fair price.

- **Independence of Decision Making:** All buyers and sellers are fully independent. None of them is committed to anyone. Hence, the buyers are free to purchase the required commodity from any seller and sellers are free to sell their commodity to any buyer or buyers. The price of a commodity at a particular time tends to be equal all over the market which all the firms have to follow.

- **Absence of Selling and Transportation Costs.** It is assumed that selling and transportation costs have no role to play in the determination of price.

5.3.3 PRICE UNDER PERFECT COMPETITION

We can analyse the equilibrium of a firm under Perfect Competition in both the short-run as well as in the long run.

A. SHORT RUN EQUILIBRIUM OF A FIRM UNDER PERFECT COMPETITION

Under short period, the firm can face four different situations depending on whether:

- AR > AC   Supernormal Profits

- AR = AC   Normal profits

- AR < AC   Losses

- AR < AC < AVC   Shut down point

a)   **Supernormal Equilibrium:** E is the point of stable equilibrium as MC = MR and the MC cuts the MR from below.

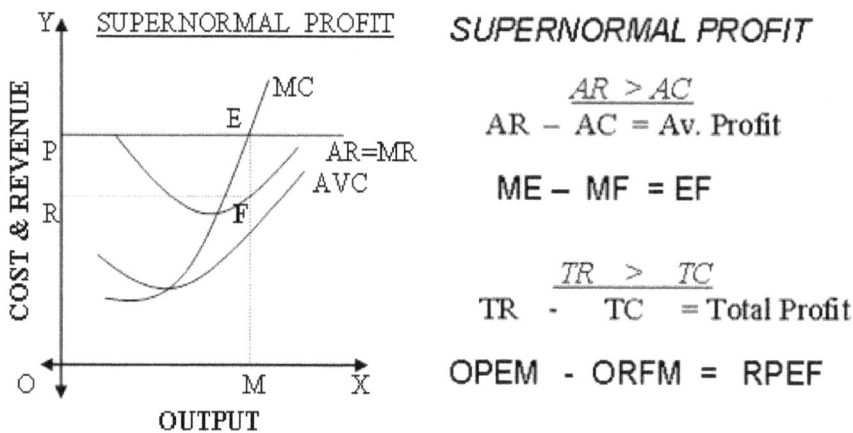

Fig. 5.1: Supernormal Equilibrium

This is point the firm produces OM amount of the output. To produce this output, the firm incurs an average cost of MF, while it earns average revenue of ME. Since at equilibrium ME > MF, the firm makes a profit of FE per unit of output sold. Again, since the total revenue earned when OM is sold is OPEM and the total cost incurred to produce the same output is ORFM, the total profit earned at that level of output is RPEF.

b) **Normal Profits:** With the condition of MC = MR and the MC cuts the MR from below, if E is the point of stable equilibrium, output of the firm is OM. produce this output, the firm incurs an average cost ME, while it earns average revenue, which is also equal to ME. Thus, we see that the firm just makes a normal profit – i.e., its AR = AC. Since the total revenue earned and the total cost incurred at output OM is OPEM, the firm earns a normal profit.

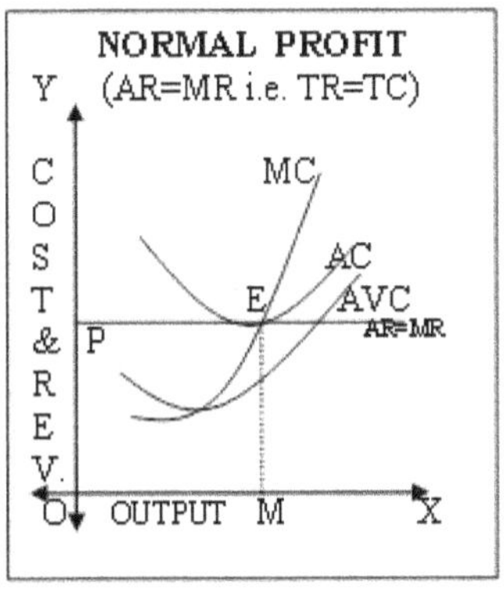

NORMAL PROFIT
(AR=MR i.e. TR=TC)

NORMAL PROFIT
□ AR = AC
AR − AC = Av. Profit

ME − ME = Zero

□ TR = TC
TR − TC = Total Profit

Fig 5.2: Normal profit equilibrium

c) **Losses:** At the point of equilibrium i.e. E where MR = MC, the firm produces OM amount of the output. To produce this output, the firm incurs an average cost of PF, while it earns average revenue, which is equal to ME. Since at equilibrium MF > ME, (AR<AC) the firm incurs a loss of EF per unit of output produced. Again, since the total revenue earned when OM output is sold is only OPEM, while the total cost incurred at output OM is ORFM, the firm incurs a total loss of PRFE. This is actually the situation of the firm minimising its losses.

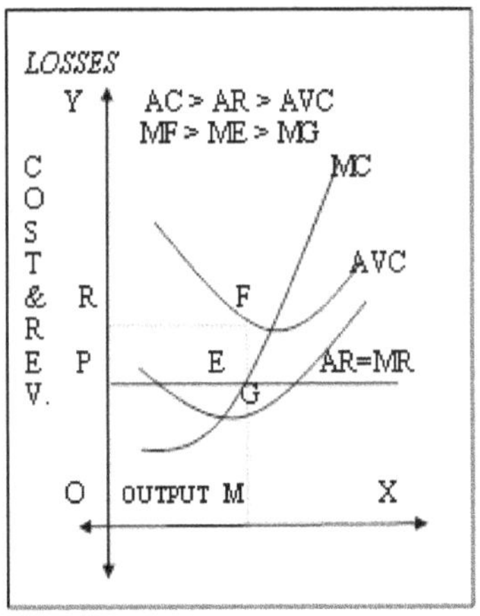

LOSSES
AC > AR > AVC
MF > ME > MG

LOSSES
□ AR < AC
AR − AC = Av. Profit

ME − MF = - EF

□ TR < TC
TR − TC = Total Profit
OPEM - ORFM = - PRFE

Fig. 5.3: Losses

In-spite of incurring loss, the firm could continue its functioning since its Average Variable Cost is being covered. At output OM, the firm covers its AVC, which is equal to MG. Hence, as long as the firm is recovering at least its AVC, it would be possible for this firm to continue functioning.

d)   Shut Down Point: With MR = MC, the firm attains equilibrium at point E where, it produces OM amount of the output. To produce this output, the firm incurs an average cost of MF, while it earns average revenue ME. At equilibrium MF > ME, the firm incurs a loss of EF per unit of output produced. Since the total revenue earned is only OPEM, while the total cost incurred is ORFM, the firm incurs a total loss of PRFE. The loss incurred is too much for this firm to continue, as this firms' AVC curve is also above its AR = MR curves – i.e. it is unable to cover even its AVC. In the above situation, at output OM, the firm's AVC, is equal to MG, which is greater than the AR = ME. Hence, this firm is not even recovering its daily or running expenses, so it should shut down.

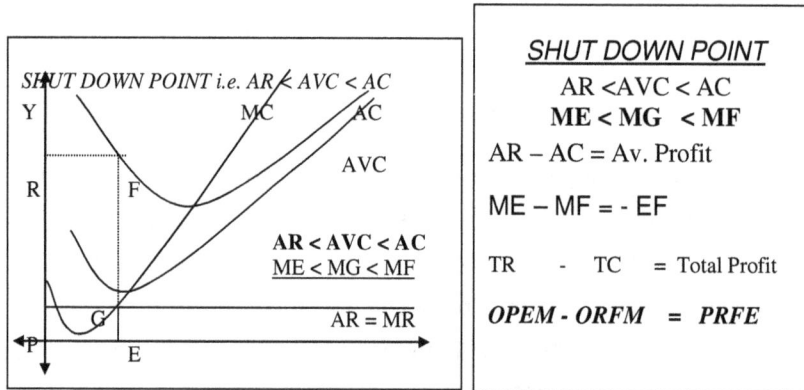

Fig. 5.4: Shut down point

B. Long Run Equilibrium of a firm under Perfect Competition

In the long run, due to the assumption of free entry and exit of the firms, it is not possible for the firms to make super-normal profits nor is it possible for them to incur losses. Hence, due to the size of the industry increasing or decreasing in the long run, firms can only earn normal profits in this time period.

The possibility of only normal profits can be explained as under.

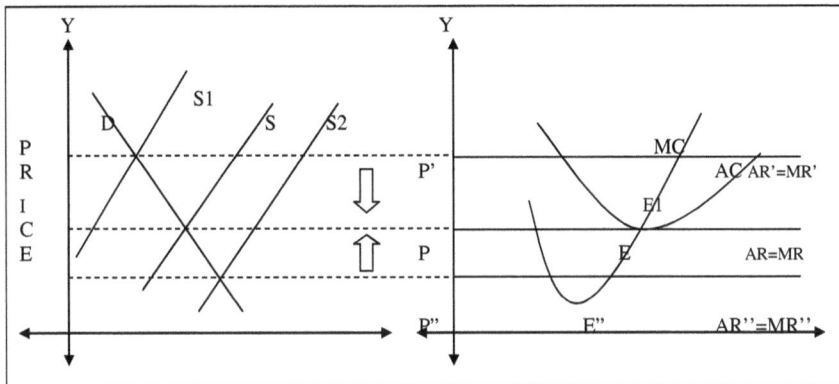

Fig. 5.5: Long Run Equilibrium under Perfect Competition

Suppose that the firm is earning a super-normal profit in the long run, since the industry's price (OP) (i.e. the firm's AR' = MR' = OP') is greater than its AC. In this situation, new firms would find this area of production to be attractive and hence they would enter this industry in large numbers. With the number of firms increasing, the supply in the industry also rises. As the supply rises, the price will start lowering. This will go on until the supply curve becomes S1 to S. This leads to fall in price from P' to P. The firm's AR=MR curve becomes tangential to the firms LAC at point E and so from the situation of earning super-normal profits the profit's size has been reduced to normal profit.

Suppose that the firm is incurring losses in the long run since the industry's price (OP) (i.e. the firm's AR'' = MR'' = OP'') is lower than its AC. In this situation, some of the firms that are unable to recover even their AVC will shut down and leave the industry. With the number of firms decreasing, the supply in the industry also falls. As the supply keeps falling, the price will start rising. Thus, price rises from P'' to P. This will go on until the supply curve becomes S2 to S. The firm's AR=MR curve becomes tangential to the firms LAC and so from the situation of incurring losses, the firm's revenues have improved so as to convert losses into normal profits.

Hence, we can conclude that in the long run, a firm under perfect Competition can only earn normal profits and not earn super-normal profits or incur losses.

⚠	**Study Notes**

5.4 Monopoly

The term 'Monopoly' has been derived from Greek term 'Monopolies' which means a single seller. Thus, monopoly is a market condition in which there is a single seller of a particular commodity who is called monopolist and has complete control over the supply of his product.

5.4.1 DEFINITION OF MONOPOLY

1. Prof. Thomas   "Broadly, the term Monopoly is used to cover any effective price control, whether of supply or demand of services or goods; narrowly it is used to mean a combination of manufacturers or merchants to control the supply price of commodities or services".

2. Prof. Chamberlain   "Monopoly refers to the control over supply".

3. Prof. Robert Triffin   "Monopoly is a market situation in which the firm is independent of price changes in the product of each and every other firm".

He is called a monopolist. He is the only producer in the industry. There are no close substitutes for his product. Thus, when there is only one seller of a commodity and there is no competition at all, the situation is one of pure monopoly.

A monopolist firm is itself an industry, for the distinction between a firm and an industry disappears under monopoly.

In technical language, pure monopoly is a single firm-industry where the cross-elasticity of demand between its product and the products of the other industries is zero.

Professor E.H. Chamberlin points out that the essence of monopoly is control over supply.

Pure monopoly rarely exists in reality. It is merely a theoretical concept, because even if there were no close substitutes, some kind of competition would always be there, such as a choice between decorating a house or buying a car. However, even though pure monopolies are a rare phenomenon in developed countries, they are found in developing countries like India in the form of State monopolies, e.g. the Mahanagar Telephone Nigam Ltd. (MTNL) and the Post and Telegraph Department of the Government of India.

5.4.2 CHARACTERISTICS OF MONOPOLY

From the above discussion, let us summarise the main characteristics of monopoly as under:

- There is a single producer of a commodity.

- There is absence of competition.

- There are no close substitutes for a monopoly product.

- Cross-elasticity of demand for a monopoly product is zero in the case of pure monopoly and very low in the case of simple monopoly.

- The monopolistic firm has control over supply of its commodity.

- There is no distinction between firm and industry under monopoly.

- Cases of pure monopolies are not found in developed countries. However, such cases of pure monopolies are found in developing countries.

- A monopolist will prevent entry of new firms in the long run.

5.4.3 TYPES OF MONOPOLY

- **Natural Monopoly:** Natural monopoly is due to natural factors. For example, a particular raw material is concentrated at a particular place and this gives rise to monopoly exploitation of such material, e.g. monopoly of diamond mines in South Africa.

Bangladesh has monopoly of raw jute.

- **Public Utility Monopoly:** Governmental authorities seize complete control and management of some utilities to protect social interests. For example, posts and telegraph, telephones, electric power, railway transport, provision of water, are monopolies of the government and local authorities. There may be private monopolies of public utility services.

- **Fiscal Monopoly:** To prevent exploitation of employees and consumers, government nationalises certain industries and acquires fiscal monopoly power over them. E.g. Fiscal monopoly of tobacco in France, Life insurance and general insurance monopoly in India

- **Legal Monopoly:** Some monopolies are engendered and protected under certain laws. Inventors of new processes, articles or devices obtain monopoly powers for such inventions under patent, trade mark and copyright laws. There are many examples of legal monopoly of medicines. As Professor F.W. Taussing observes in his *Principles of Economics,* copyrights and patents are the simplest cases of absolute monopoly by law. However, as Professor E.H. Chamberlin points out, such cases would fall more under monopolistic competition than under monopoly.

- **Voluntary Monopoly through Combinations:** To eliminate competition and thereby secure higher prices, firms producing a particular product may come together and make monopoly agreements. These are known as industrial combinations. When all the firms merge into one organisation, such a monopoly takes the form of a trust. The Associated Cement Companies (A.C.C.) in India is an example of this kind of trust. Where the firms maintain their individual identity and yet enter into monopoly agreements such combinations are known as trade associations, pools, cartels and holding companies. A pool is deemed a loose combination to maintain a particular higher price level of a commodity. A cartel is based on agreements to restrict output to get high prices e.g. the Sugar Syndicate in Maharashtra. A holding company secures monopolistic control over a number of firms by holding a majority of shares in them.

5.4.4 SOURCES OF MONOPOLY

- **Legal Sanction:** A monopoly as stated above may be the result of a government sanction. The government of a country may legally permit a private monopoly or monopoly in the public sector for myriad reasons. National security (e.g. manufacture of defense equipments), social equity (post office, water supply, electricity supply, telephones) or economic considerations (public utility services or essential goods to be produced on a large scale by a single firm for reducing the cost and price e.g. monopoly of transport services) are paradigms of such monopolies. Monopolies may be created to avoid wastes due to duplication of services e.g. public utilities.

- **Control Over Supply of Inputs:** Secondly, a monopoly situation may arise due to control over the supply of an essential input - raw materials, skilled labour, technology used-denying access to these inputs to any potential firm e.g. government monopoly of Railways in India. Rail tracks are not used by private rail companies. Monopolies may be protected through a protectionist policy of the government by putting tariffs on foreign goods.

- **Merger for Large-scale Production:** Thirdly, monopoly undertaking may be a consequence of the necessity to produce on a large scale to reduce costs. Existing small firms may merge into a big firm or may not survive in the long period. It is only when there is single firm in such a situation that costs are greatly reduced due to the economies of large-scale production.

- **Rival Firms Eliminated:** Fourthly, pressure tactics and unfair means by a giant firm may lead to elimination of rival firms from the industry to secure sole position of a giant firm. In India, many such examples were revealed in the Monopoly Inquiry Commission's report.

5.4.5 PRICE UNDER MONOPOLY

The aim of the monopolist is to maximise profit therefore; he will produce that level of output and charge that price that gives him maximum profits. He will be in equilibrium at that price and output at which his profits are the maximum. In other words, he will be in equilibrium position at that level of output at which marginal revenue equals marginal cost. In order to achieve equilibrium, the monopolist should satisfy two conditions:

- Marginal cost should be equal to marginal revenue.

- The marginal cost curve should cut marginal revenue curve from below.

A. Short run equilibrium of a firm under monopoly

The short run equilibrium of the monopolist is shown below in figure 5.6.

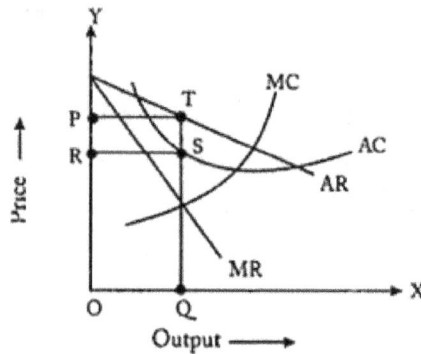

Fig. 5.6: Abnormal Profit under Monopoly

AR is the average revenue curve, MR is the marginal revenue curve, AC is the average cost curve and MC is the marginal cost curve. Up to OQ level of output marginal revenue is greater than marginal cost but beyond OQ the marginal revenue is less than marginal cost. Therefore, the monopolist will be in equilibrium where MC=MR. Thus, a monopolist is in equilibrium at OQ level of output and at OP price. He earns abnormal profit equal to PRST.

However, it is not always possible for a monopolist to earn super normal profits. If the demand and cost situations are not favourable, the monopolist may incur short run losses.

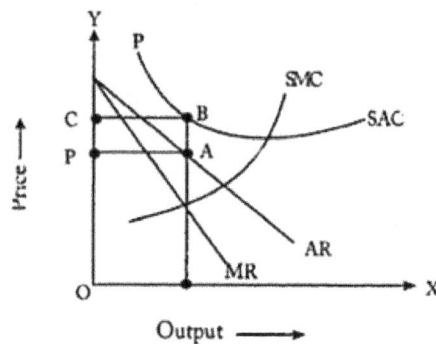

Fig. 5.7: Loss under Monopoly

Though the monopolist is a price maker, due to weak demand and high costs, he suffers a loss equal to PABC as shown above in figure 5.7.

B. Long run Equilibrium of a Firm under Monopoly

In the long run, the firm has the time to adjust his plant size or to use the existing plant so as to maximise profit. The long run equilibrium of the monopolist is shown in figure 5.8.

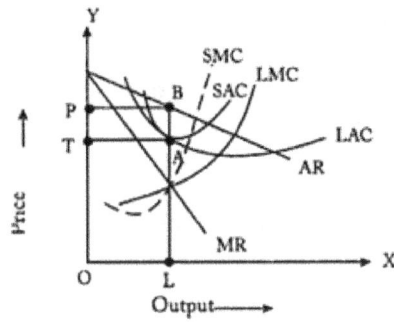

Fig. 5.8: Long run equilibrium of a firm under monopoly

The monopolist is in equilibrium at OL output where LMC cuts MR curve. He will charge OP price and earn an abnormal profit equal to TPQH.

⚠	**Study Notes**

👁	**Assessment**
1.	Explain Monopoly Market structure.
2.	Explain features and types of Monopoly.

🗣	**Discussion**
Discuss Pricing under Monopoly.	

5.5 Monopolistic Competition

In the real world, market is neither perfectly competitive nor a monopoly. The great majority of imperfectly competitive producers in the real world produce goods, which are neither completely different nor completely same. They produce goods, which are analogous to those produced by their rivals. This means that the goods produced in the market are close substitutes. It follows that such producers must be concerned about the way in which the action of these rivals affects their own profits. This kind of market is known as 'monopolistic competition' or group equilibrium. Here there is competition, which is keen, though not perfect, between firms manufacturing very similar products, for example market for toothpaste, cosmetics, watches, etc.

5.5.1 FEATURES OF MONOPOLISTIC COMPETITION

Following are the features of a monopolistic competitive market:

- **Large number of firm:** Monopolistic competition is characterised by large number of firms producing close substitutes but not identical product. Each firm must control a small yet significant portion of the market share such that by substantially extending or restricting its own sales, it is not able to affect the sales of any other individual seller. This condition is the same as in perfect market.

- **There is product differentiation:** No seller has full control over the market supply. Each seller produces very close substitute products. The product is neither identical nor markedly different. Since every seller produces slightly differentiated product, each seller has minor control over the price. Unlike perfect market conditions, the firm is a price – maker to some extent. That is, a firm can change the price slightly, though not much. The control over price will depend on the degree of product differentiation.

- **Absence of Inter-dependence:** Existence of a large number of firms insures the condition too large and too small. Thus, the individual firm's supply is small constituent of total supply. Therefore, individual firm has limited control over price level. Similarly, each firm can decide, its price or output policies independently through price discrimination, any action by one firm may not invite reaction from rival firms.

- **Selling cost:** Competitive advertisement is an essential feature of monopolistic competition. Selling cost becomes an integral part of the marketing of firms when product is differentiated. It is necessary to tell the buyers about the superiority of the product and induce the customer to buy the products.

- **Free entry and exit:** Under monopolistic competition, new firms can enter or existing firms can exit. There are no restrictions on entry or exit. Moreover entry is easy because of the small size of firms. Existence of supernormal profit attracts entry and existence of loss, business firms to quit the market.

5.5.2 ASSUMPTIONS OF MONOPOLISTIC COMPETITION

- There are a significant number of sellers as well as buyers in the 'group'.

- Products of the sellers are separated, however they are close substitutes of one another.

- There is free entry as well as exit of the organisation in the group.

- The objective of the firm is to maximise profits, both in the short run as well as in the long run.

5.5.3 PRICE DETERMINATION UNDER MONOPOLISTIC COMPETITION

A) SHORT-TERM EQUILIBRIUM OF A FIRM

Short-term implies to the period where a firm is not able to regulate the supply of its product as per the demand. Owing to this reason, a firm is not able to accomplish much taking into account its profit situation in the short-run. Thus, in the short-run, there could be three contingencies concerning profit (i) Abnormal profit, (ii) Normal or Zero profit, (iii) Loss.

1. **Abnormal Profit.** In short-run an organisation could be capable of acquiring abnormal profit only as soon as the demand of the organisation's product is extremely high and there is no close substitute to its product. Under these circumstances, the organisation can establish a high price for its product and can acquire abnormal profit. This can be achievable only in the short-run, as no new organisation can become involved in the market in the short-run. It can be explained with the help of figure 5.9.

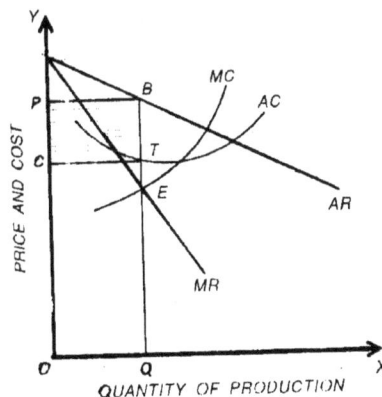

Fig. 5.9: Supernormal Profit under Monopolistic Market

In the figure above, 'E' is the point of equilibrium of firm because at this point marginal cost and marginal revenue of the firm are equal. At this point 'OP' is the equilibrium price, OQ is the equilibrium quantity of production and sale, PC is the profit per unit. In this situation, the firm is earning abnormal profit equal to the area PBTC.

2. **Normal Profit or Zero Profit:** If the demand of the organisation's product is not extremely high, the organisation could acquire only normal profit once average revenue is a little more than the average cost or zero profit as soon as average revenue and average cost are equal. These situations can be explained with the help of figure 5.10.

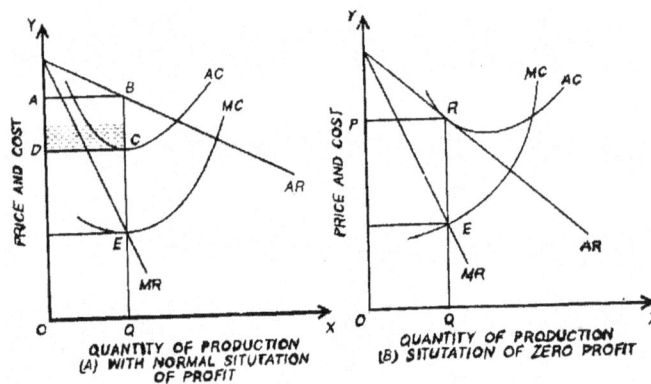

Fig. 5.10: (A) Normal Profit and (B) Zero Profit under Monopolistic Competition

In the figure 5.10 (A) above, 'E' is the point of equilibrium of firm because at this point marginal cost and marginal revenue of the firm are equal. At this point, 'OQ' is the equilibrium quantity, 'OA' is the price per unit and 'OD' is the cost per unit. Here, average revenue is slightly more than average cost; in this case, the firm accrues profit equal to the area of 'ABCD'.

In the figure 5.10 (B) above, 'E' is the point of equilibrium of firm because at this marginal cost and marginal revenue of the firm are equal. At this point, 'OQ' is the equilibrium quantity, 'OP is the price per unit and 'OP' is also the cost per unit. Here, average revenue and average cost are equal. Therefore, the firm is not making any profit or loss.

3. **Loss:** In short-run, a firm may have to suffer loss when demand of the product of firm is so weak that the firm has to sell its product at a price less than its cost, in this case, average revenue of the firm is less than its average cost. It can be illustrated with the help of figure 5.11 given below:

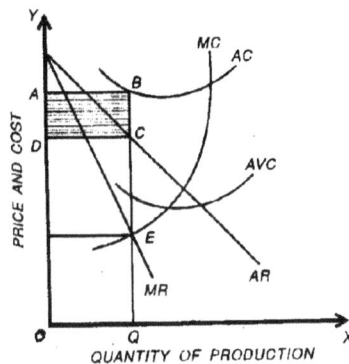

Fig. 5.11: Loss under Monopolistic Market

In the figure 5.11 above, average revenue of the firm is less than its average cost. 'E' is the point of equilibrium. At this point, 'OQ' is the equilibrium quantity, 'OD' is the price per unit and 'OA' is the cost per unit. Here, price per unit is less than cost per unit. Therefore, the firm is suffering a loss equal to the area ABCD.

B) Long-term Equilibrium of a Firm

Long-term is the period where an organisation could regulate the supply of its product as per its demand. It is the period where new organisations can furthermore become involved in the market. In this situation, an organisation at all times acquires normal profit, as in case an organisation is acquiring abnormal profit in short-term, new organisations will become involved in the market. It will add to the supply of the product and consequently the price of the product will decline. This series of new organisations getting involved in the market will carry on till the organisation is in the position of acquiring normal profit only. In contrast, if an organisation is suffering a loss in the short-run, several organisations will leave the industry. In this situation, supply of the product will decline and price of the product will rise to the level of average cost or a little more than the average cost. Consequently, the organisation will acquire normal profit. Nevertheless, following two conditions should be fulfilled for the equilibrium of an organisation in the long-run.

- Marginal cost as well as marginal revenue of all the organisations should be equal.

- Average cost as well as average revenue of all the organisations should be equal.

It can be explained with the help of the following figure

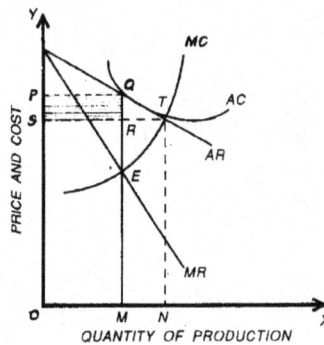

Fig. 5.12: Long run Equilibrium under Monopolistic Market

In the figure 5.12 mentioned above, 'E' is the point of equilibrium. At this point, MC = MR. At this point, 'OM' is the equilibrium quantity, 'OP' is the equilibrium price and 'QM' is the average cost. At this point, average cost and average revenue are equal. It satisfies the conditions of normal profit. In this situation, the firm is accruing normal profit equal to the area of PQRS.

5.5.4 DEFECTS OR WASTES OF MONOPOLISTIC COMPETITION

EXCESS CAPACITY

It implies the amount of output by which the long run output of the firm under monopolistic competition falls short of the Ideal output. This is considered as wastage in monopolistic competition.

The excess capacity under imperfect competition emerges because of downward sloping demand curve. It can be tangent only at the falling part of LAC. This means the greater the elasticity of this downward sloping demand curve, lesser will be excess capacity.

A firm under monopolistic competition in long run equilibrium produces an output, which is less than what is deemed socially optimum or ideal output. Society's productive resources are fully utilised when they produce the output at minimum long run average cost. However, firm under monopolistic competition operates at the output on the falling portion of LAC; which implies it is not operating at minimum LAC point. However, under perfect competition the firm in long period operates at minimum LAC i.e. Ideal output or socially optimum output.

- **Unemployment:** Under imperfect competition, the production capacity of the firm is not used fully. This implies that there is underutilisation of capacity. This leads to unemployment.

- **Exploitation:** Under imperfect competition the output is restricted, so that price is kept higher than the marginal cost (AR>MC). The excess of the price on MC represents real extra burden on the community i.e. exploitation. Under perfect competition this exploitation is not possible as price is equal to AC and MC (AR=MC=AC)

- **Advertisement:** Expenditure on competition advertisement is regarded as a waste of competition. It is the result of imperfect competition because under perfect competition there is no need for such advertisement due to homogenous products. However, under imperfect competition product is differentiated and therefore advertisement becomes necessary in order to earn larger share in the market.

- **Cross Transport:** The existence of cross transport is another factor contributing to waste of imperfect competition. A firm in India may be a selling a commodity in India while the same product produced in India may be sold abroad. This is also the result of absence of perfect competition and presence of product differentiates.

- **Specialisation:** Another waste of imperfect competition is the failure of each firm in India to specialise in the production of those commodities for which it is best suited.

- **Standardisation:** Under imperfect competition, standardisation which helps in reducing cost is not possible. No produce can take the rich producing particular design on larger.

⚠	**Study Notes**

👁	**Assessment**
1.	Explain Monopolistic Market structure in detail.
2.	What are the defects and wastages of Monopolistic Market structure.

Discussion
Discuss Pricing under Monopolistic Competition.

5.6 Oligopoly

The type of market condition, which is most appropriate in the today's economy, is oligopoly. It is characterised by mutual interdependence among a few sellers who control the total market supply. Oligopoly, therefore, occurs when there are only a few sellers. It differs from both monopoly and perfect competition and from monopolist competition. Oligopoly is a market where a small group of producers, have significant control over major portion of the market demand, with or without differentiated product.

5.6.1 DEFINITION OF OLIGOPOLY

Mrs. John Robinson- "Oligopoly is market situation in between monopoly and perfect competition in which the number of sellers is more than one but is not so large that the market price is not influenced by any one of them".

Prof. George J. Stigler- "Oligopoly is a market situation in which a firm determines its marketing policies on the basis of expected behaviour of close competitors".

Prof. Stoneur and Hague- "Oligopoly is different from monopoly on one hand in which there is a single seller, on the other hand, it differs from perfect competition and monopolistic competition also in which there is a large number of sellers. In other words, while describing the concept of oligopoly, we include the concept of a small group of firms".

Prof. Left Witch- "Oligopoly is a market situation in which there are a small number of sellers and the activities of every seller are important for others".

Thus, oligopoly is a market situation in which a few firms producing an identical product or the products, which are close substitutes to each other, compete with each other.

5.6.2 CHARACTERISTICS OF OLIGOPOLY

Oligopoly can be characterized as follows:

- **Small Number of Sellers:** There are more than one sellers of a product however; the number is not so huge in order to generate perfect competition of monopolistic competition.

- **Interdependence of Sellers:** All the sellers are dependent on each other. They are not free to establish their own marketing and price policies. Activities of one seller have an effect on others.

- **Homogenous product:** The product of all the sellers is identical or a close substitute to each other.

- **Uniformity of Price:** All the sellers adopt a uniform price policy due to the uniformity of their product.

- **Price Rigidity:** As the activities of all sellers are inter-reliant, the sellers prefer not to change the price of their product too often. For that reason, the market price happens to be steady.

- **Entry and Exit of Firms:** The entry as well as exit of organisations is relatively difficult because of non-availability of raw materials, labour, etc.

- **Inconsistency in Firms:** All the organisations operating in a market are not precisely similar to each other. One organisation could be huge and another organisation could be tiny.

- **Uncertainty of Demand Curve:** Demand curve is extremely erratic. An organisation cannot predict its demand curve without difficulty because it is extremely difficult to predict whether or not the competitors will change their policies of the organisations. It is moreover extremely difficult to predict the level of such changes. For this reason, the demand curve of an oligopoly organisation is constantly erratic.

5.6.3 PRICE-OUTPUT DETERMINATION UNDER OLIGOPOLY

(Kinky Demand Curve) Short Period

The kinked demand curve was first employed by Prof. Paul M. Sweezy to explain price rigidity under oligopoly. In an oligopoly market, the firm knows that if it increases price, other firms will not follow; but if price is reduced, other firms will follow the price reduction. In some respect, the price output analysis in oligopoly is simple. Since each seller wants to avoid uncertainty, every oligopolistic firm will adhere to the point of kink, where it

Managerial Economics

is safe and where it can anticipate the reaction of its rivals. However, the firm will neither increase nor decrease price.

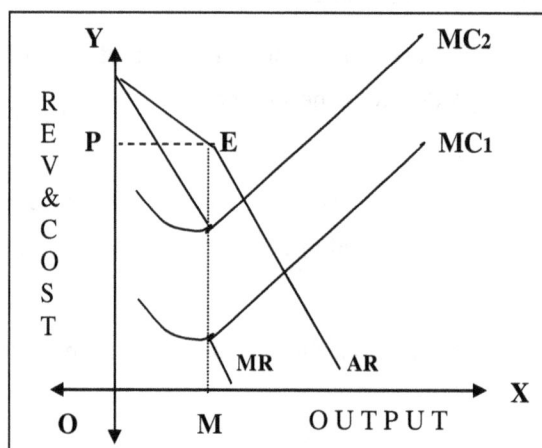

Fig. 5.13: Kinked Demand Curve

This is an important consequence of the existence of the kink in the demand curve of the firm. Because, of the vertical section in MR, i.e. uncertainty range, without affecting the price or level of output. Under these circumstances, equality between MC and MR will not determine the point of equilibrium. The profits will, however, be determined as in any other market, by the difference between AR and AC. With a given marginal cost of production, OP is more likely to be the profit-maximising price. The length of the discontinuity portion in the MR depends on the relative elasticity of demand at point E of AR. The greater the elasticity of demand of the portion of AR above point E and the lower the elasticity of demand of the portion of AR below point discontinuity portion of MR, the bigger will be the discontinuity portion of MR. Figure 5.16 shows that the price is fixed at OP and output is OM.

🔔	**Study Notes**

👁	**Assessment**

1. Define Oligopoly

2. What are the features of Oligopoly

3. Explain types of Oligopoly.

🗣	**Discussion**

Give practical examples of Oligopoly Market situation.

5.7 Summary

Market economy pricing is conditioned by the market structure. There are many different market structures. Perfect competition is accorded great importance as a market structure by the classical and neoclassical economists.

Types of market structures formed by the nature of competition:

- Traditionally, the nature of competition is adopted as the fundamental criterion for distinguishing different types of market structures.

- The degrees of competition may vary among the sellers as well as the buyers in different market situations. The nature of competition among the sellers is viewed based on two major aspects: The number of firms in the market and the characteristics of products, such as whether the products are homogeneous or differentiated.

An individual seller's control over the market supply and his hand on price determination basically depends upon these two factors.

On the selling side or supply side of the market, the following types of market structures are commonly distinguished:

- Perfect competition

- Monopoly

- Oligopoly

- Monopolistic competition.

Managerial Economics   177

Perfect competition and monopoly are the two extremes of the market situations. Other forms of market such as oligopoly and monopolistic competition fall in between these two extremes. Oligopoly and monopolistic competition are the market situations characterized by imperfect competition.

PERFECT COMPETITION

Perfect Competition is a market situation where a large number of buyers as well as sellers come together to provide the similar product. They possess complete knowledge of the market, the equilibrium price everywhere in the market. The firms are free to take part in and to exit the market.

MONOPOLY

The term 'monopoly' has been derived from Greek term 'monopolies', which means a single seller. Thus, monopoly is a market condition in which there is a single seller called monopolist of a particular commodity and has complete control over the supply of his product.

Pure monopoly rarely exists. It is merely a theoretical concept because even if there were no close substitutes, some kind of competition would always be there, such as a choice between decorating a house or buying a car. However, even though pure monopolies are a rare phenomenon in developed countries, they are found in developing countries like India in the form of State monopolies e.g. the Mahanagar Telephone Nigam Ltd. (MTNL) and the Post and Telegraph Department of the Government of India.

MONOPOLISTIC COMPETITION

In the real world, market is neither perfectly competitive nor a monopoly. The great majority of imperfectly competitive producers in the real world produce goods, which are neither completely different nor completely same. They produce the goods, which are similar to those produced by their rivals. This implies that the goods produced in the market are close substitutes. It follows that such producers must always be concerned about the manner in which the action of these rivals affects their own profits. This kind of market is known as 'monopolistic competition' or group equilibrium. Here there is competition, which is keen, though not perfect, between firms producing very similar products, for example market for toothpaste, cosmetics, watches etc.

OLIGOPOLY

The type of market condition, which is realistic in present day economy, is oligopoly. It is characterised by mutual interdependence among a few sellers who control the total market supply. Oligopoly, therefore, occurs when there are only a few sellers. It differs from both the monopoly and perfect competition and also from monopolist competition. Oligopoly is a market where a small group of producers, have significant control over major portion of the market demand, with or without differentiated product.

5.8 Self Assessment Test

Broad Questions:

1. What are the characteristics of perfect competition? What is the relative position of a firm in a perfectly competitive industry? How does it choose its price and output?

2. Under what market conditions is a firm a price-taker. What would happen to a firm if it becomes price-maker?

3. Write a note on "The Relationship between average revenue and marginal n under (i) perfect competition and (ii) monopoly".

4. For a profit maximising monopoly, price is greater than marginal cost and it n so over a large range of output. Why does then a monopolist not produce when MC = MR?

5. A monopoly firm may earn normal or abnormal profits or may even incur in the short-run. Do you agree with this statement? Give reasons for your answer.

Short Notes

   a. Importance of AR, AC, MR and MC in determining firm equilibrium under perfect competition.

   b. Oligopoly and Price determination under Oligopoly

   c. Differentiate between Monopoly and Monopolistic Competition

   d. Price determination under Perfect competition for Long as well as short run.

   e. Monopoly and types of Monopoly

5.9   Further Reading

1. A Modern Micro Economics, Koutsoyiannis, Macmillan, 1991

2. Business Economics, Adhikary, M,., Excel Books, New Delhi, 2000

3. Economics Theory and Operations Analysis, Baumol, W J., 3rd ed., Prentice Hall Inc, 1996

4. Economics Organisation and Management, Milgrom, P and Roberts J, Prentice Hall Inc, Englewood Clitts, New Jersey, 1992

5. Managerial Economics, Chopra, O P., Tata McGraw Hill, New Delhi, 1985

6. Managerial Economics, Keat, Paul G and Philips K Y Young, Prentice Hall, New Jersey, 1996

7. Managerial Economics, Maheshwari, Yogesh, Sultanchand and Sons, 2009

8. Managerial Economics, Varshney, R L. Sultanchand and Sons, 2007

Managerial Economics

Assignment

Give two examples of each: Perfect Market, Monopoly, Monopolistic and Oligopoly Market practiced in your area.

_____

_____

_____

_____

_____

_____

_____

_____

_____

_____

_____

_____

_____

_____

_____

_____

_____

_____

_____

_____

_____

_____

Glossary

Absolute advantage   A country has an absolute advantage if its output per unit of input of all goods and services produced is higher than that of another country.

Aggregate demand   is the sum of all demand in an economy. This can be computed by adding the expenditure on consumer goods and services, investment and not exports (total exports minus total imports).

Aggregate supply   is the total value of the goods and services produced in a country, plus the value of imported goods less the value of exports.

Average total cost   is the sum of all the production costs divided by the number of units produced.

Balance of Payment   is the summation of imports and exports made between one country and the other countries with which it carries out trade.

Balance of trade   The difference in value over a period between a country's imports and exports

Barter system   System where there is an exchange of goods without involving money

Break even   A term used to describe a point at which revenue equals cost. (Fixed and variable)

Budget   It is a summary of intended expenditures along with proposals for how to meet them. A budget can provide guidelines for managing future investments and expenses.

Budget deficit   The amount by which government spending exceeds government revenues during a specified period of time usually a year

Capital budget   It is a plan of proposed capital outlays and the means of financing them for the current fiscal period. It is usually a part of the current budget. If a capital program is in operation, it will be the first year thereof. A capital program is sometimes referred to as a capital budget.

Capital Budgeting	To make investment decisions that will maximise the value of the firm
Capital	It refers to wealth in the form of money or property owned by a person or business and human resources of economic value. Capital is the contribution to productive activity made by investment is physical capital (machinery, factories, tools and equipments) and human capital (eg general education, health). Capital is one of the three main factors of production; other two are labour and natural resources.
Cartel	An organisation of producers seeking to limit or eliminate competition among its members, most often by agreeing to restrict output to keep prices higher than would occur under competitive conditions. Cartels are inherently unstable because of the potential for producers to defect from the agreement and capture larger markets by selling at lower prices.
Centrally planned economy	A planned economic system in which the production, pricing and distribution of goods and services are determined by the government rather than market forces is referred to as a planned economy or a 'non market economy'. Former Soviet Union, China and most other communist nations are examples of centrally planed economy
Classical economics	The economics of Adam Smith, David Ricardo, Thomas Malthus and later followers such as John Stuart Mill
	The theory concentrated on the functioning of a market economy, spelling out a rudimentary explanation of consumer and producer behaviour in particular markets and postulating that in the long term the economy would tend to operate at full employment

because increases in supply would create corresponding increases in demand.

Closed economy	A closed economy is one in which there are no foreign trade transactions or any other form of economic contacts with the rest of the world.
Cost benefit analysis	A technique that assesses projects through a comparison between their costs and benefits, including social costs and benefits for an entire region or country. Depending on the project objectives and its the expected outputs, three types of CBA are generally recognised: financial; economic; and social. Generally, cost-benefit analyses are comparative, i.e. they are used to compare alternative proposals. Cost-benefit analysis compares the costs and benefits of the situation with and without the project; the costs and benefits are considered over the life of the project.
Cost-Volume-Profit-Analysis	It is the volume of output, which equates TR and TC.
Cross elasticity of demand	The change in the quantity demanded of one product or service affecting the change in demand for another product or service. E.g. percentage change in the quantity demanded of a good divided by the percentage change in the price of another good (a substitute or complement)
Deflation	Deflation is a reduction in the level of national income and output, usually accompanied by a fall in the general price level.
Duopoly	A market structure in which two producers of a commodity compete with each other
Econometrics	The application of statistical and mathematical methods in the field of economics to test and quantify economic theories and the solutions to economic problems
Economic Cost	Explicit Cost + Implicit Cost

Economic development	The process of improving the quality of human life through increasing per capita income, reducing poverty and enhancing individual economic opportunities
	It is also sometimes defined to include better education, improved health and nutrition, conservation of natural resources, a cleaner environment and a richer cultural life.
Economic growth	An increase in the nation's capacity to produce goods and services
Economic infrastructure	The underlying amount of physical and financial capital embodied in roads, railways, waterways, airways and other forms of transportation and communication plus water supplies, financial institutions, electricity and public services such as health and education. The level of infrastructural development in a country is a crucial factor determining the pace and diversity of economic development.
Economic integration	The merging to various degrees of the economies and economic policies of two or more countries in a given region
Economic policy	A statement of objectives and the methods of achieving these objectives (policy instruments) by government, political party, business concern etc
	Some examples of government economic objectives are maintaining full employment, achieving a high rate of economic growth, reducing income inequalities and regional development inequalities and maintaining price stability. Policy instruments include fiscal policy, monetary and financial policy and legislative controls (e.g., price and wage control, rent control).
Economic Profit	Total Revenue-Economic Cost
Economics of Scope	It occurs when the joint production cost is less than the cost of producing multiple outputs separately.

Economics	The art of applying economic theory in business and administrative decision making
Elasticity of demand	The degree to which consumer demand for a product or service responds to a change in price, wage or other independent variable
	When there is no perceptible response, demand is said to be inelastic.
Excess capacity	Volume or capacity over and above the required amount, to meet peak planned or expected demand
Excess demand	Situation in which the quantity demanded at a given price exceeds the quantity supplied- Opposite: excess supply
Expected Value of Profit	It is the values of the profits weighed by the underlying probability distribution.
Fixed costs	A cost incurred in the general operations of the business that is not directly attributable to the costs of producing goods and services. These 'fixed' or 'indirect' costs of doing business will be incurred whether or not any sales are made during the period, thus the designation 'fixed', as opposed to 'variable'.
Gross domestic product (GDP)	Gross Domestic Product: The total of goods and services produced by a nation over a given period, usually 1 year
	Gross Domestic Product measures the total output from all the resources located in a country, wherever the owners of the resources live.
Gross national product (GNP)	It is the value of all final goods and services produced within a nation in a given year, and income earned by its citizens abroad, minus income earned by foreigners from domestic production. The fact book, following current practice, uses GDP rather than GNP to measure national production. However, the user must realise

Managerial Economics

that in certain countries net remittances from citizens working abroad may be important to national well being. GNP equals GDP plus net property income from abroad.

Human capital Productive investments: Investments embodied in human persons. These include skills, abilities, ideals and health resulting from expenditures on education, on-the-job training programs and medical care.

Imperfect competition A market situation or structure in which producers have some degree of control over the price of their product e.g. monopoly and oligopoly

Imperfect market A market where the theoretical assumptions of perfect competition are violated by the existence of, for example, a small number of buyers and sellers, barriers to entry, non-homogeneity of products and incomplete information

The three imperfect markets commonly analysed in economic theory are monopoly, oligopoly and monopolistic competition.

Income inequality The existence of disproportionate distribution of total national income among households whereby the share going to rich persons in a country is far greater than that going to poorer persons (a situation common to most LDCs). This is largely due to differences in income derived from ownership of property and to a lesser extent the result of differences in earned income. Inequality of personal incomes can be reduced by progressive income taxes and wealth taxes. This is measured by the Gini coefficient.

Inflation Percentage increase in the prices of goods and services

Internal Rate of Return It is the discount rate, which equates the present value of the expected cash flow to the initial cost of investment.

International commodity agreement Formal agreement by sellers of a common internationally traded commodity (coffee, sugar) to coordinate supply to maintain price stability

International poverty line An arbitrary international real income measure, usually expressed in constant dollars (e.g., $270), used as a basis for estimating the proportion of the world's population that exists at bare levels of subsistence

Learning Curve When knowledge gained, experience is used to improve production techniques, which results in a decline in the long-run average cost.

Long-run Cost It is when the time is long enough to change all inputs therefore all costs are variable.

Macroeconomics The branch of economics that considers the relationships among broad economic aggregates such as national income, total volumes of saving, investment, consumption expenditure, employment and money supply. It is also concerned with determinants of the magnitudes of these aggregates and their rates of change over time.

Market economy A free private-enterprise economy governed by consumer sovereignty, a price system and the forces of supply and demand

Market failure A phenomenon that results from the existence of market imperfections (e.g., monopoly power, lack of factor mobility, significant externalities, lack of knowledge) that weaken the functioning of a free-market economy--it fails to realize its theoretical beneficial results. Market failure often provides the justification for government interference with the working of the free market.

Market mechanism The system whereby prices of stocks and shares, commodities or services freely rise or fall, when the buyer's demand rises or falls or the seller's supply of them decreases or increases

Market prices	Prices established by demand and supply in a free-market economy
Market-friendly approach	World Bank notion that successful development policy requires governments to create an environment in which markets can operate efficiently and to intervene selectively in the economy in areas where the market is inefficient (e.g., social and economic infrastructure, investment coordination, economic 'safety net')
Microeconomics	The branch of economics concerned with individual decision units--firms and households--and the way in which their decisions interact to determine relative prices of goods and factors of production and how much of these will be bought and sold. The market is the central concept in microeconomics.
Mixed economic systems	Economic systems that is a mixture of both capitalist and socialist economies
	Most developing countries have mixed systems. Their essential feature is the coexistence of substantial private and public activity within a single economy.
Monopoly	A market situation in which a product that does not have close substitutes is being produced and sold by a single seller.
Open economy	It is an economy that encourages foreign trade and has extensive financial and nonfinancial contacts with the rest of the world in areas such as education, culture and technology.
Opportunity Cost	It is often known as implicit cost or non-cash cost. It is the fore-gone cost associated with current next best use of an asset.
	The implied cost of not doing something that could have led to higher returns.
Perfect competition	A market situation characterized by the existence of very many buyers and sellers of homogeneous goods or

services with perfect knowledge and free entry so that no single buyer or seller can influence the price of the good or service

Political economy
The attempt to merge economic analysis with practical politics- to view economic activity in its political context

Much of classical economics was political economy and today political economy is increasingly being recognised as necessary for any realistic examination of development problems.

Price elasticity of demand
The responsiveness of the quantity of a commodity demanded to a change in its price, expressed as the percentage change in quantity demanded divided by the percentage change in price

Price elasticity of supply
The responsiveness of the quantity of a commodity supplied to a change in its price, expressed as the percentage change in quantity supplied divided by the percentage change in price

Price
It is the monetary or real value of a resource, commodity or service. The role of prices in a market economy is to ration or allocate resources in accordance with supply and demand; relative prices should reflect the relative scarcity of different resources, goods or services.

Revenue expenditure
This is expenditure on recurring items, including the running of services and financing capital spending that is paid for by borrowing. This is meant for normal running of governments' maintenance expenditures, interest payments, subsidies, transfers etc. It is current expenditure, which does not result in the creation of assets. Grants given to State governments or other parties are also treated as revenue expenditure even if some of the grants may be meant for creating assets. Subsidy: Financial assistance (often from the

Managerial Economics

	government) to a specific group of producers or consumers
Revenue receipts	Additions to assets that do not incur an obligation that must be met at some future date and do not represent exchanges of property for money Assets must be available for expenditures. These include proceeds of taxes and duties levied by the government, interest and dividend on investments made by the government, fees and other receipts for services rendered by the government.
Short -run Cost	It is when the time is not enough to change all inputs; therefore, costs are classified into fixed and variable costs
Sunk Cost	The cost that does not change or vary across decision alternatives
The Value of the Firm	The PV of the expected future net cash flows discounted by the appropriate discount rate

www.ingramcontent.com/pod-product-compliance
Lightning Source LLC
Chambersburg PA
CBHW082309210326
41599CB00029B/5748